The Elements of the Case Interview

A training program to develop problem-solving skill and habits of communication that are above the bar

Manu Lakshmanan, Ph.D.

Published in the United States of America
ISBN # 9798692683236

Dedicated to my mom, Sushila Lakshmanan

Everything should be made as simple as possible,
but not simpler.

– Albert Einstein

Table of Contents

Acknowledgements

Numerous contributors are responsible for this book in its current form.

Deepti Reddy, Geoffrey Abraham, Kedar Karkare, Pavida Charoen-Rajapark, Phoebe He, Vincent Lai, and Yaying Feng reviewed early drafts of the manuscript in its entirety and provided insightful feedback. Their suggestions greatly strengthened the text for the target audience of case interview candidates. I am grateful for their generosity.

My editor, Daniele Ellis; indexer, Obajuwana Anne Onajite; graphical designer, Muhammad Awais Yousaf; and type-setter, Andrea Reider, all brought painstaking attention to detail to ensure the quality of the text and did so with a sense of humor.

Finally, my many case practice partners, mentors and clients at McKinsey & Company, and case interview coaching clients taught me the ideas presented in this text and were therefore my inspiration for this project.

Foreword

It was September 2018 and I had been struggling to progress beyond first-round management consulting interviews for 4 months. I decided to google "consulting coaching" and came across Manu Lakshmanan. A few weeks after engaging Manu's coaching services, I was offered a consultant role at McKinsey & Company, which I gladly accepted.

I had been pursuing roles in management consulting for many of the same reasons as do most: to gain exposure to public and private sectors, to build a new skill-set in efficient problem solving, and to work on solving some of the most pressing and large scale challenges in healthcare and social sector (my expertise) in the world. And, as a medical doctor, with both employment history and a masters from Harvard University, I hoped that with a bit of independent case practice I'd have an offer for a consulting role in no time.

However, I had just been knocked back from another interview- this time at BCG- and I was utterly disappointed. I was sure that I, like many people, had the intrinsic ability to be a management consultant (after all, no-one goes to university for 4 years to study management consulting!). But in working alone, I had not yet mastered the learnable techniques of case interviews. It was clear to me that, if I were to land a consulting offer, I needed some tailored coaching and guidance from someone experienced, and with a track record of coaching people into consulting roles. Manu was this person.

Needless to say, after a few highly clarifying coaching sessions with Manu and 7 interviews later, I landed a role in McKinsey & Company. I was informed by a partner who interviewed me that I "blitzed" my interviews. How, in only a few sessions, had Manu enabled me to perform at a standard I had not been able to achieve alone in more than 4 months working alone? Here's what I learned from Manu:

1. **Be methodical.** Manu gave highly tailored and precise coaching on how to work through case interview problems systematically, allowing me to stay organized and communicate more clearly when solving a case.
2. **Be specific.** Particularly when it came to the personal interview, Manu showed me how to extract meaningful details from my personal stories to best illustrate how I was the right person for the role.
3. **Practice alone.** Manu encouraged me to interpret graphs, perform back-of-the-envelope calculations and structure problems alone, which was critical for improving my performance.
4. **Relax and have fun.** Being relaxed and confident in my abilities enabled me to think more clearly through problems, and conduct myself in a relaxed way that instilled trust by the interviewer.

I learned a great deal about consulting and case-interviews from Manu's coaching. Manu helped me to better understand the consulting mindset, and to feel confident in my own intrinsic abilities (which, quite frankly, is half the battle). I am grateful for all I learned during my time as a management consultant, and Manu's coaching played a significant role in allowing me that opportunity. I could not recommend his insights more highly.

Simone Sandler, MBBS MPH BMedSc(Hons)
Medical Doctor
Harvard University Masters of Public Health
McKinsey and Company Alumnus, Australia
Currently working in strategy in the pharmaceutical industry
September 29th, 2020

CHAPTER 1

The Onsight Case System®

"Those times when you get up early and you work hard; those times when you stay up late and you work hard; those times when you don't feel like working, you're too tired, you don't want to push yourself, but you do it anyway; that is actually the dream. That's the dream. It's not the destination, it's the journey." – Kobe Bryant at his jersey retirement ceremony [1], December 18, 2017

I chose this quote from Kobe Bryant because the case interview preparation process that you are experiencing now is the beginning of what could be one of the most rewarding learning journeys of your life. My objective in this book is to provide case interview candidates an exhaustive review of the principles for the problem-solving process that management consultants apply on the job and that are therefore tested in the case interview.

The Problem-Solving Process and accompanying intra-team communication involved in that process has become ingrained in the way I approach my work every day. In fact, the diagram of the 7-Step Problem-Solving Process that I will introduce to you is hanging in my office even now. When my company CEO has a request for analysis to help him make a strategic decision, I am the go-to person because he knows that I will quickly provide an exhaustive analysis. I am able to do that because I define the problem (the strategic question) precisely, use an issue tree, and prioritize issues. These skills came from my case interview training.

I hope that you approach your case interview preparation not as a set of esoteric tips and tricks that you will only use for a day to pass the job interview only to never use again. Instead, I hope that you invest the focus and effort warranted to developing skills that you will use every minute once you're on the job in consulting and in your post-consulting career.

What that means for you is that you should approach this process in the same way you approach learning any other lifelong skill. Put in the long hours, reflect on your strengths and weaknesses, and revisit your plans on how to improve.

Section 1-1 Sources of the approach described in this book

Here I've aspired to lay out an exhaustive but prescriptive approach to succeed in the case interview. My goal is that you can use this book as a complete handbook for case interview preparation. The approach to preparing for the case interview presented in this book is based on:

- my two journeys through the consulting interview process—one unsuccessful, one successful—and the contrast between those two experiences;
- coaching over 400 candidates from varying backgrounds through the consulting interview process over the last 6 years;
- my experience as a consultant serving clients in consulting engagements and interviewing candidates at McKinsey, living the firm's values and applying its Problem-Solving Process in individual and team scenarios.

The first time I went through the consulting interview process, I did not receive a consulting offer. I did not know how my life would unfold because I would soon defend my PhD without a job offer in hand. Ironically, a little over a year later when I received a consulting offer, I actually put in less effort the second time around. The differentiating factor in that second attempt was that I was more deliberate in my practice, a concept that I will describe in more detail in Section 8-1 and Section 9-5.

Since working at McKinsey, I've enjoyed serving as a case interview coach. One of my practices as a coach to help me identify trends in a candidate's performances over time is to maintain structured notes from every coaching session. When I sat down to write this book, I scraped through my notes from well over 2,000 case interview coaching sessions that I've conducted to synthesize the most common mistakes I see candidates make and the challenges that they face when preparing for the case interview. I've endeavored to address these common issues here so you can manage them.

My case interview skills improved further while at McKinsey because consultants use case interview skills every minute on the job. I've based my coaching philosophy—and therefore the approach laid out in this book—on pushing my case interview clients to solve problems the same way consultants do. You'll notice language used in this book about what a consultant communicates to a consulting client or senior partner as a reference point for how you should communicate with your interviewer.

Section 1-2 Introduction to the case interview

The case interview tests your problem-solving skills interactively. It is a unique problem-solving dialogue that takes place between two people using a hypothetical client problem (called a "case"). Therefore, the two key components of the case interview are problem-solving and communication. The dialogue and phases of the case interview are designed to simulate, on a much shorter time scale, the types of scenarios you will face as a consultant over the course of a typical client-facing project. These conversations follow a predictable format, which is as follows.

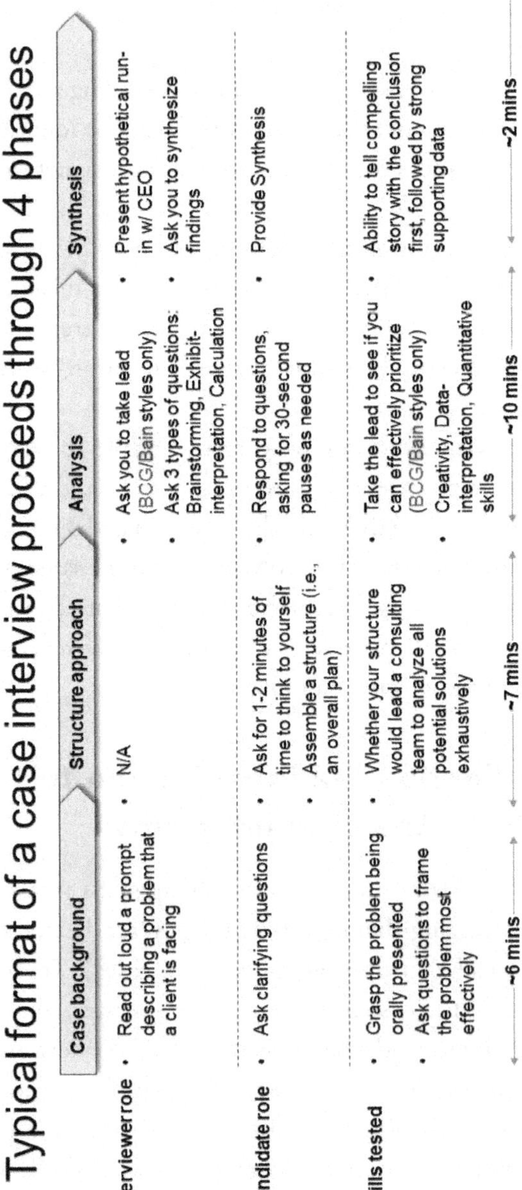

Typical format of a case interview proceeds through 4 phases

	Case background	Structure approach	Analysis	Synthesis
Interviewer role	• Read out loud a prompt describing a problem that a client is facing	• N/A	• Ask you to take lead (BCG/Bain styles only) • Ask 3 types of questions: Brainstorming, Exhibit-interpretation, Calculation	• Present hypothetical run-in w/ CEO • Ask you to synthesize findings
Candidate role	• Ask clarifying questions	• Ask for 1-2 minutes of time to think to yourself • Assemble a structure (i.e., an overall plan)	• Respond to questions, asking for 30-second pauses as needed	• Provide Synthesis
Skills tested	• Grasp the problem being orally presented • Ask questions to frame the problem most effectively	• Whether your structure would lead a consulting team to analyze all potential solutions exhaustively	• Take the lead to see if you can effectively prioritize (BCG/Bain styles only) • Creativity, Data-interpretation, Quantitative skills	• Ability to tell compelling story with the conclusion first, followed by strong supporting data
	~6 mins	**~7 mins**	**~10 mins**	**~2 mins**

Figure 1-1 Typical structure of a case interview.

The interviewer will kick off by reading you a prompt describing a problem that a client is facing and needs your help to solve. Your ability to grasp the problem and then ask appropriate questions to frame it most effectively is the first skill you'll be tested on.

Then it is customary for you as the interviewee to ask for 1-2 minutes of time to think as you assemble a structure (i.e., an overall plan) for how you'll approach the problem. The structure that you present will be evaluated by the interviewer for whether it would lead a consulting team to analyze all potential solutions exhaustively and efficiently over the course of the project.

After you present your structure, in the interviewee-led format (discussed in greater detail in Section 2-9) that is used by BCG and Bain, the interviewer will then ask you something to the effect of "Where would you like to start?" Your ability to take the lead at this point will be evaluated to see if you can effectively prioritize the different components in the case. You will be asked similar questions such as "What would you like to learn about next?" a few more times in this interviewee-led format, further probing your ability to prioritize issues.

In both the interviewee-led format and interviewer-led format used by McKinsey, the interviewer will make sure to expose you to a few preplanned questions:

- Math, e.g., "Can you calculate...?"
- Brainstorming, e.g., "What are all the ways in which our client could...?"
- Exhibit-interpretation, e.g., "Here is some data the client shared with us. Based on this, can you tell me...?"

These categories of questions test your quantitative ability, your creativity, and your ability to discern recommendations from data.

Finally, towards the end of the interview, the interviewer will abruptly ask you to provide a hypothetical client CEO (or another senior leader at the client) with an update. Here you're being tested for your ability to bring together the disparate quantitative and qualitative findings throughout the conversation to weave into a story or key message to present to the client.

Let's now discuss how you can train to perform at a sufficiently high level on the case interview.

Section 1-3 Introduction to the System

Based on the need to develop an understanding of problem-solving and communication in the case interview, and the practice needed to translate that understanding into skill, I've developed a 3-pillar preparation system. In Figure 1-1, I lay out these 3 pillars:

1. **Problem-solving:** the fundamental skill tested, and one that you will use every hour of every day once you become a consultant. In Part I, I will introduce you in depth to the type of problem-solving that consultants use on the job. If you apply the same problem-solving process in the case interview that consultants use in client engagements, you will succeed.
2. **Habits of communication:** In addition to general problem-solving skills, you also need to prepare your communication skills for the specific style of dialogue in the case interview. In Part II, we discuss how to approach communication to do well on the case interview.
3. **Training:** as with all skills, you cannot succeed with theoretical understanding alone. In Part III, I lay out a training regimen that you should follow to develop your skills to the level needed to receive a consulting offer.

Figure 1-1 The Onsight Case System® 3-pillar approach—used to coach hundreds of case interview candidates to consulting offers—to develop skill level to pass the final round of case interviews.

Section 1-4 How much time and effort will this process require?

You can expect your case interview preparation to take between 1 to 4 months, with 11.5 to 25 hours per week of effort as broken down in Figure 1-2. Where you land on this spectrum will depend on how much time you allot and your skill level coming into this process. I will discuss how to customize your preparation plan in more detail in the next section (Section 1-5).

Sufficient case interview preparation requires 11.5 to 25 hours per week of deliberate practice over 1 to 4 months

Phase	Preparation category	Drill	Sessions per week	Time per session (min)	Total time (hrs)
Intro: 1-time investment	Read a book or review video lectures on case interviews as an introduction to the concepts involved		N/A	N/A	3.5-4.5
Weekly training: 1-4 months	Scrimmages: partner cases	Mock case interviews as the interviewer	2-5	45	1.5-3.8
		Mock case interviews as the interviewee	2-5	45	1.5-3.8
	Working out and training	Flash cards review	4-8	15	1-2
		Structuring exercise using business periodical	10-14	15	2.5-3.5
		Brainstorming exercise using business periodical	10-14	15	2.5-3.5
		Exhibit interpretation exercise using casebook	2-6	15	0.5-1.5
		Math exercise using casebook	3-10	30	1.5-5.0
		Final recommendation exercise using casebook	2-6	15	0.5-1.5
Total weekly commitment					**11.5-24.6**

Figure 1-2 Action plan to prepare for case interview and time estimate.

The exercises laid out in this plan will be described in detail in Part III. This plan is a general guideline. We will discuss how you should design a custom plan that's optimal for you in Section 8-1 and Section 9-5.

Section 1-5 Starting points: MBA vs non-MBA's

Candidates from a wide variety of educational backgrounds interview for consulting roles and face the case interview. Does it matter whether your education background covered business training? Do MBA's have an advantage?

It's much like preparing to take the SAT or ACT in your senior year of high school after taking pre-calculus in your junior year. (For international audiences not familiar with the SAT/ACT, it is a college admission exam in the United States that covers content including algebra and geometry). Having those additional math courses beyond the level of math covered in the SAT and ACT is not helpful because those subjects aren't tested. But if your coursework has exposed you to those advanced concepts, then you are more likely to have memorized key concepts tested on the SAT (i.e., rules of algebra and geometry) and are more likely to appreciate those concepts. Those two characteristics will improve your SAT performance. However, test-takers who have not taken pre-calculus can develop those two characteristics by spending more time memorizing formulas and by developing an appreciation for math.

When we think of this analogy for the case interview, candidates without business coursework may be less likely to have memorized the key business concepts (e.g., concepts in mergers and acquisitions); and are less likely to enjoy discussing business. Regarding the second point, non-business candidates from engineering backgrounds are less likely to enjoy the creative qualitative parts of the case interview like brainstorming and structuring qualitative questions. Non-business candidates from humanities backgrounds, on the other hand, are less likely to enjoy the math questions on the case interview.

So if you don't have a business background, how can you mitigate these two issues so you can perform as well as someone with a business background? I will explicitly discuss these concerns in Section 8-2 in the chapter on training.

Let's now turn to a prescriptive guide for the most important skill tested in the case interview: problem-solving.

PART I

Problem-solving

CHAPTER 2

Seven-step problem-solving approach

"Our problems are manmade—therefore, they can be solved by man.... For peace is a process—a way of solving problems."–John F. Kennedy, Commencement Address at American University, June 10, 1963 [4]

Section 2-1 The type of problem-solving tested in the case interview

Where the behavioral interview tests your soft skills (such as leadership, influencing skill, and entrepreneurial drive), the case interview tests your problem-solving skill. But there are so many categories of problems we face that require different problem-solving approaches that the skill of "problem solving" is too broad to have much specific meaning. Therefore, in this chapter, we define the specific type of problem solving that consultants use, which you therefore need to focus on developing to succeed at the case interview.

To understand this contrast, consider that each of these situations that require problem-solving:

- a political leader mitigating the risk of nuclear war
- a rock climber choreographing a sequence of movements to ascend a boulder problem
- a researcher in a hard science setting up an experiment to test a theory
- a physician diagnosing a patient and formulating a treatment plan
- a social scientist gathering empirical data to test or develop a theory
- a lawyer preparing a case to prosecute an alleged criminal
- a mathematician or physicist proving a theorem

Would Kennedy, Einstein, or a rock climber perform well on the case interview based on their political-, physics- or choreography-based problem-solving skill? Probably not, for reasons we turn to now.

The differentiating factors unique to the type of problem solving that consultants practice are:

1. **Quantitative considerations:** consultants need to support recommendations with quantitative analysis foremost.
2. **Qualitative considerations:** taking into account risks, management-related considerations, uncertainty of external environment, and so on are important analyses that a consultant needs to account for in their recommendations.
3. **Data availability limitations:** whereas a scientist can generate as much data as needed by designing and running experiments, in business we cannot observe how scenarios will play out in a test tube or simulation.
4. **Timeline limitations:** when businesses bring in consultants, they are looking for results quickly, and consultants need to

deliver on that expectation. This kind of time pressure does not exist in academic disciplines, and therefore consultants cannot and should not do as many deep dives as an academic.

5. **Accuracy tolerance permitted:** in academic disciplines, the research community expects scientists to only publish rigorously tested results that are statistically significant using the Student's t-test or other statistical hypothesis testing methods. It is worthwhile for a scientist to take as much time as needed to achieve that kind of accuracy. Businesses (and by extension their consultants), by contrast, need to manage the tradeoff between accuracy and timeliness to adapt to fast-changing markets.
6. **Communication requirement:** much like a researcher needs to explain their research method and logic to their audience in a publication, a consultant needs to explain the rationale behind their recommendations convincingly to their clients. However, many problem-solving disciplines don't require the problem-solver to communicate their rationale. Michael Jordan need not explain his logic behind deciding to not pass the ball, and Steve Jobs need not explain the logic behind launching the iPhone—the results in both cases speak for themselves.

Table 2-1 summarizes how the differentiating aspects of problem-solving in consulting compare and contrast with those of other disciplines.

#	Differentiating aspect of consulting	Disciplines that share this aspect	Disciplines that do not share this aspect
1	Quantitative considerations	hard sciences; math; medicine; business	political science; sports
2	Qualitative considerations	medicine; political science; business; sports; law	hard sciences; math
3	Data availability limitations	social sciences; business; law	hard sciences; math
4	Timeline limitations	business; medicine; law	academic disciplines
5	Accuracy tolerance is lenient	sports; political science; business; law	academic disciplines; medicine
6	Communication requirement	academic disciplines; business; medicine; law	sports

Table 2-1. Comparing and contrasting the 6 differentiating aspects of the problem-solving required in consulting with other problem-solving disciplines.

What are the implications of these defining characteristics for how a consultant should approach problem solving? To answer that question, we now turn to McKinsey's 7-Step Problem-Solving Approach.

Section 2-2 McKinsey 7-Step Problem-Solving Approach

To optimize its ability to solve its clients' challenges while working around the defining characteristics laid out in the previous section, McKinsey & Company articulated to its consultants a 7-Step Problem-Solving Process that it has also shared publicly [5], [6]. In Figure 2-1, I lay out this 7-step problem-solving process with brief titles and sub-headings for each step.

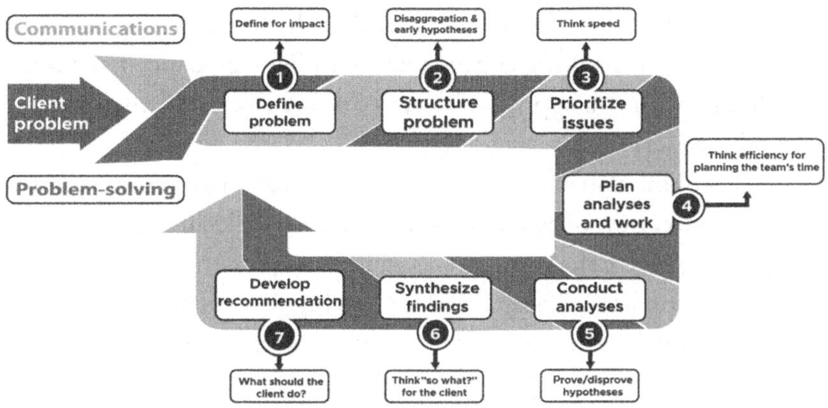

Figure 2-1 McKinsey 7-step problem solving method [1], [2].

McKinsey specifically designed and optimized this 7-Step Process for the features laid out in Table 2-1. Notice that given the need to incorporate both *qualitative* and *quantitative data* (the first and second aspects from Table 2-1), there are explicit steps for disaggregating these components (Step 2: "Structure problem") and rolling up all the different analyses (Step 6: "Synthesize Findings").

There is a step to "Prioritize issues" (Step 3) to ensure that the consulting team can maximize impact given the *timeline limitations* and to take advantage of the *accuracy tolerance* available (the fourth and fifth aspects from Table 2-1). To manage the genuine challenge of data availability limitations, there is an explicit step to "Plan analysis" (Step 4). To ensure that the thinking of the consulting team is *communicated* to the client (the sixth aspect from Table 2-1), McKinsey explicitly defined each of these 7 steps in the problem-solving process so that the team can share it in a tangible or communicable form with the client.

Consulting firms are looking to see how you can solve problems relative to how their consultants do. Can you conduct end-to-end analyses with light guidance from senior consultants? Are you a smart, quick, and independent thinker who formulates clear hypotheses and structures portions of the consulting engagement with light guidance from senior consultants? Can you apply the 7 steps of the Problem-Solving Process as a thought leader?

At this point, you may think each of the 7 steps may map to one stage of the case interview or that at least you need to walk through the 7 steps in sequence to solve the case. However, it's not quite that simple. To clarify how you apply the 7-Step Problem-Solving Process in your interview, let's walk through each stage of the case interview.

Section 2-3 Clarifying questions

You're in the final round of interviews with the consulting firm of your dreams, and the partner has just read you the prompt about a fictional client that you scribble onto your sheet of paper. Your mind goes blank and you have no idea what the solution to this problem could be. What's worse, you do not know this industry.

Stay calm and trust the 7-Step Problem-Solving Process, which McKinsey designed for consultants facing all sorts of problems, many of which are vastly different from problems or industries they've dealt with before.

<u>Step 1: Define Problem</u>. Start at the top with Step 1: "Define problem." A useful framework for defining a problem is the one you're encouraged to use anytime you set a goal: set SMART goals. Setting a SMART goal for your client engagement means that it is:

1. **S**pecific: let's be clear on the objective(s) for our client engagement. Is it to determine whether to enter a market? And/or is it to determine how to enter the market? Clarify the objective(s), be as specific as possible, write it at the top of your first slide, and put a box around it.

2. **M**easurable: what KPI (key performance indicators) or metrics mean the most to the client that they will use to measure success? Is it revenue, profit, ROI, or NPV? Clarify that with your interviewer.
3. **A**ttainable: what KPI target value would define success for this client? Do they just want to get profits growing again or do they have a more ambitious profitability target that they want to hit? We want to under-promise and over-deliver.
4. **R**elevant: this point is unnecessary for you. The interviewer will always select relevant problems for the case interview.
5. **T**ime-bound: when does the client need to hit their desired KPI goal(s)? Is it okay if our plan involves making investments in year 1 that causes them to have negative profitability as long as it gets them to profitability in year 2? We need to understand the timeline because it will inform our strategy.

A frequent mistake I see during this part of the case interview is the interviewee asking something like "is there any other information that you can share?" You need to remember that you are the thought leader and there is infinite information available in a consulting engagement: publicly available SEC documents, the worldwide web, Google, the knowledge of the employees at the client, experts within your consulting firm that you can interview and so on. More information is available from paid sources: subscriptions, expert interviews, databases maintained by research firms, and so on.

As the thought leader, it's your job to identify what information is worth spending the time and/or money retrieving, so don't ask your client or the senior partner on the project what information you need. It's your job to lay out an approach, and their job to provide feedback and suggestions based on your thoughts.

Section 2-4 Developing your structure for the overall case

Perhaps the most nerve-wracking part of the whole case: you ask for some time to develop an approach for the client's problem and the unspoken 2-minute clock ticks for you to develop the perfect MECE (i.e., mutually exclusive, collectively exhaustive—a concept we will cover in Chapter 3) structure for this client-problem while the interviewer watches you. Chapter 3 discusses strategies for structuring problems, so here I want to highlight the relevant steps from the 7-Step Problem-Solving Process that relate to structuring.

Although it may seem that this part maps only to the Structuring step (Step 2) of the 7-Step Problem-Solving Process, providing examples of Steps 3 and 4 (Prioritize Issues and Plan Analyses) strengthens your structure by illuminating the branches of your structure. Let's touch on how to incorporate each of these 3 steps (Steps 2 through 4) during the Structuring stage.

Step 2: Structuring the problem. When structuring the problem, the problem-solving team breaks it down into a manageable set of parts (e.g., "revenue" and "costs" for a profitability-focused project) for the purpose of organizing its approach (e.g., assigning certain parts to specific team members). Chapter 3 contains structure visualizations.

Step 3: Prioritize issues. When presenting your structure, it's helpful for the problem-solving team and the audience to have a general understanding of the relative importance of these parts of the structure (e.g., do we think 80% of the value will come from revenue or costs?). Give your interviewer a taste of how you'd prioritize the components in your structure as a way to show that you've already started forming hypotheses.

Step 4: Plan analyses. When you present your structure, you are also sharing a plan for how you will tackle this big hairy problem. It's helpful to give the interviewer or your audience a taste of the kinds of analysis you will conduct within each component part of your structure. That is valuable commentary for them to understand your structure. Keep it brief, however; they can ask for more detail if they're interested.

Section 2-5 Brainstorming questions

In the McKinsey or interviewer-led format of the case interview, the interviewer will ask you a series of questions. In the interviewee-led format used by firms such as BCG and Bain, the interviewer will expect you to ask them questions to get the information you need. In the latter, if you laid out a MECE hypothesis-driven prioritized structure, you will have elicited the data you need from your interviewer, and it becomes equivalent to the interviewer-led scenario for the subsequent question.

When the interviewer asks a brainstorming question related to the case, you aren't being asked to develop any recommendations, so you don't have to work through all 7 steps of the Problem-Solving Process. Instead, you are being asked to create a list of ideas that the team can further investigate to make a recommendation later. That means you need to work through the process until the "Plan Analyses" step:

1. Confirm that you understand the question and have defined the goals. (Define Problem).
2. Develop a structure to come up with the broadest, most thorough set of brainstormed solutions. (Structure the Problem).
3. Share which bucket you think will drive the most impact for the client. (Prioritize issues).
4. Brainstorm a list of ideas under each bucket of your structure that we can later investigate. You need not develop a full plan to investigate each idea, just the list of ideas. (Plan analysis—partially).

We'll discuss more specific concrete examples of this approach for brainstorming questions in Section 4-3.

Section 2-6 Exhibit-interpretation questions

The interviewer slides a piece of paper in front of you with complex data charts on it and asks you for your thoughts. While the interviewer watches you, you need to cut through the noise in the chart and identify the most important insights in the data. Because you are being asked to translate the exhibit into what it means for the client (i.e., for the recommendations you will make), you need to step through all 7 steps of the Problem-Solving Process. This is where many interviewees go wrong by making random irrelevant observations or asking random questions ("Do we have any information on...?").

Let's slow it down and walk through the 7 steps:

1. Confirm our objective here. Did the interviewer ask for you to do anything in particular with this exhibit, or is the objective the same as the overarching objective for the case? Let's clarify that and write it at the top of our fresh sheet of paper. (Define the problem).
2. What structure do we want to apply that can serve as a checklist of items we want to scour this exhibit for (e.g., let's search the exhibit for revenue opportunities and cost opportunities in a profitability case)? This often can be our overarching structure for the case or the rows/columns of the exhibit itself, but if the interviewer asked you a more specific question for this exhibit, tweak that structure a bit for that specific question. (Structure problem).
3. Be aware of what the top priority items in your structure are. (Prioritize issues).
4. Instead of "planning analyses," we need to understand the analysis that was done since the exhibit shows analyses that have already been completed. Let's make sure we understand what analyses or method was used to assemble the data that this exhibit contains. E.g., how was the y-axis calculated? (Plan analyses).
5. Now let's scour the exhibit for the items in our structure and extract all insights we observe. (Conduct analyses).

6. Let's take inventory of these insights we've uncovered and synthesize what this means for our client. (Synthesize findings).
7. If we're not at a stage to make a recommendation to the client, then develop an action plan (i.e., a list of analyses to conduct next) for what we need to do to get to a point where we can develop a recommendation. (Develop recommendation).

The most common mistake I see when interviewees interpret exhibits is not extracting enough insights, which you can improve upon by stressing Step 2. I will walk through an example of how to apply this approach to interpreting exhibits in Section 4-4.

Section 2-7 Quantitative questions

Now the interviewer is giving you quantitative data and asking you to do a complex calculation without a computer or calculator while they stare at you. Again, you are being asked to conduct an analysis and translate it into what it means for the client, so instead of asking for random pieces of data, step through all 7 steps of the Problem-Solving Process:

1. Be specific about the objective of this calculation, e.g., what units does the interviewer want the eventual answer in (dollars or number of customers)? Write it at the top of a fresh sheet of paper and put a box around it. (Define Problem).
2. Share your planned method to do this calculation and get feedback from your interviewer. (Structure the Problem).
3. Identify which parts of the methodology (such as which customer segments) are most important. (Prioritize issues).
4. Identify what data sources you'll use to get any additional numbers you may need, such as publicly available financial documents or by interviewing employees at the client. (Plan analyses).
5. Crunch the numbers by doing the actual calculation on your paper. (Conduct analyses).
6. Translate what your calculated number means for the client. (Synthesize findings).

7. If you're not at a stage to make a recommendation to the client, then develop an action plan for what you need to do to get there. (Develop recommendation).

A common mistake I see on math questions in the case interview is the interviewee finishing the calculation, presenting their final answer (Step 5) and believing that they have sufficiently answered the question—forgetting Steps 6 and 7. We'll discuss each of these steps in more specific concrete detail in Chapter 5 on Quantitative Problem-Solving.

Note that in the interviewee-led format (e.g., for BCG and Bain) that Step 7 is what enables you to drive the case forward. I want to stress that this step is just as important, however, for any consulting engagement, and therefore is necessary in the interviewer-led format.

Section 2-8 Final recommendation to the CEO

You get into the elevator and the CEO walks in before the doors close and asks you how your consulting engagement for her is going. The interviewer maybe even tells you that you have no time to collect your thoughts before responding.

This situation does map to Step 7 to develop a recommendation. However, this is more of a communication-focused scenario as you don't have time to follow any Problem-Solving Process when you're in the proverbial CEO elevator-ride. Therefore, we'll touch on how to deal with this situation in the chapter on Communication in Section 7-6.

Section 2-9 A note on Interviewer-led versus Interviewee-led formats

Some consulting firms (such as McKinsey) conduct the case interview through asking a series of questions. The interview preparation community refers to this approach as the "Interviewer-led" format. On the other hand, some consulting firms (such as BCG and Bain) conduct the case interview by asking an upfront question and then letting you lead the discussion through various stages. The community refers to this latter approach as the "Interviewee-led" format.

The two formats have more overlap than contrast. Both formats test problem-solving and communication in the same way and therefore require you to apply all the methods outlined in this book. However, there are two differences you should keep in mind with how you approach the two formats: first, anxiety of awkward silences, and second, perceived expectations.

Anxiety of awkward silences

The interviewee-led format is more nerve-wracking for you (the candidate) because the interviewer expects you to fill moments of silence. It's like filling an awkward silence on a first date. In the interviewer-led format, you don't have to deal with those awkward silences, but in the interviewee-led format, you do. There are two ways to manage this anxiety.

The first is to ingrain the habits of applying the "Prioritize issues" (Step 3) and "Develop recommendations" (Step 7) steps of the 7-Step Problem-Solving Process. When you get into the habit of prioritizing issues (Step 3), you will naturally lay out what is the most important task at hand in order to fill those awkward silences.

When you get into the habit of attempting to develop recommendations (Step 7), then you will naturally recognize if you are at a stage where you have enough data to recommend a course of action to your client or—if you're not at that stage yet—recognize gaps to be filled to make a recommendation. Recognizing those pieces of data you need will trigger another iteration of applying the 7-Step Problem-Solving Process. As we walk through the 3 categories of problem-solving and the distinct question types in those categories in the remainder of Part I, we will discuss how to apply the "Develop Recommendation" (Step 7) step of the process in more detail. For now, just keep in mind that you need to emphasize Steps 3 and 7 of the Problem-Solving Process in the interviewee-led format to mitigate anxiety.

The second way to manage the anxiety unique to the interviewee-led format is by practicing through simulated mock interviews. In Chapter 9, I lay out how to go about setting up and conducting simulated mock interviews with case practice partners. Be sure to let your case practice partners know that you'd like to practice the interviewee-led format.

Perceived expectations for distinct steps of the 7-step process

The second way in which the interviewer- and interviewee-led formats are different is regarding the perceived expectations for distinct steps of the 7-Step Problem-Solving Process. I want to emphasize the word "perceived" here. The expectations for the two processes are actually the same: all consulting firms use the case interview to test the same two skills: problem-solving and communication. You need to do an excellent job of applying all 7 steps of the problem-solving process regardless of the interview format.

But interviewees may perceive the emphasis on certain steps of the Problem-Solving Process to be different in the two formats, particularly for Steps 3 (Prioritize Issues) and 7 (Develop Recommendation) that we discussed to mitigate anxiety. In the interviewee-led format, the interviewer expects you to conduct these two steps to drive the conversation forward.

However, in the interviewer-led format, you may think that the interviewer is not requiring these two steps because they did not ask for them. For example, the interviewer may ask you to calculate a number, and you think that once you complete the calculation, you've answered the question sufficiently. That would be a costly mistake, as we'll discuss in Section 5-7 and Section 5-8, because the expectation is that consultants translate their analyses into recommendations for the client. The take-home point is that in the interviewer-led format, make it *second nature* to talk your interviewer through Steps 3 and 7 of the Problem-Solving Process (Prioritize Issues and Develop Recommendations) in response to *every question* you are asked.

Throughout the book, I will elaborate on these specific differences you need to keep in mind between the two formats. Otherwise, the skills tested and the approach you should use to prepare are the same regardless of the interview format.

Now that we've introduced the overarching Problem-Solving Process, I will dedicate the rest of Part I to the 3 distinct problem-solving skill sets tested on the case interview: analytical, conceptual and quantitative.

CHAPTER 3

Analytical Problem-Solving

"My challenge when I came back was to face the young talent, dissect their games, and show them maybe that they needed to learn more about the game...."–Michael Jordan, interview with Hoop Magazine, 1997 [7]

Analytical problem-solving is the skill of breaking down a large, complex problem into smaller pieces to better manage it. Michael Jordan used analytical problem-solving when he'd "dissect" the games of his younger opponents.

You will use this skill during the structuring part of the case interview that I introduced in Section 2-4. Therefore, this chapter will equip you with the tools you need to present effective problem structuring in your case interview. Note that the steps of the 7-Step Problem-Solving Process that come into play here are 2 through 4. Section 3-1 through Section 3-4 are the most in depth discussion of problem structuring in this book. Section 3-5 and Section 3-6 discuss how you need to apply Steps 3 and 4 of the Problem-Solving Process in the structuring part of the case interview.

Section 3-1 Upfront structuring: what interviewers are looking for (Step 2 of the 7-Step Problem-Solving Process)

The purpose of the upfront structuring part of a consulting engagement is to bound the overarching client problem into a subset of manageable pieces that can serve as a complete plan to develop a recommendation for the client. Given that it serves as the plan of analysis for the whole project, it is an important enough step of the Problem-Solving Process that the consulting team would want to receive feedback on it from the main client sponsor (e.g., the CEO) and use it as a tool to engage that person and their team in a problem-solving discussion on Day 1 of the project.

The purpose of an upfront structure has 3 important implications for what the interviewer wants in your structure during the case interview:

1. MECE: Mutually Exclusive and Collectively Exhaustive
   a. Mutually Exclusive: as much as possible, the parts of the structure should not overlap with each other in order to eliminate unnecessary redundancy in your structure that makes it less efficient. I want to stress the "as much as possible" point, however, because no structure can be perfectly mutually exclusive. Even the profitability structure has overlapping components within it as revenue and cost both depend on volume of production.
   b. Collectively Exhaustive: since this structure will also serve as the project plan for analysis, it should be complete. Are there any critical issues that the consulting team must take into account to make the best recommendation for the client that your structure doesn't cover? If so, your structure is not yet exhaustive. (Note that you can't achieve being collectively exhaustive by adding an "Other" catch-all bucket to all of your structures. That would defeat the purpose of structuring because you'd be leaving one entire portion of issues unstructured).
2. Fewer than 5 high-level components. Since one of the important attributes of an effective structure is that it must break the overarching problem into manageable components, it follows that the number of components must be a manageable one. Therefore, if your structure has over 6 high-level components, it becomes a complex laundry list of ideas, which defeats the purpose of having a structure.

3. Hypothesis-driven. The most common mistake I see with upfront structures is that candidates use it to ask a series of open-ended questions. One of the most important things you need to do when you present your structure to a senior person (such as a Partner or the client CEO) is to explain to them how you will use this structure to answer the overarching client-problem. The best way to do that is by sharing your hypothesis under each component or sub-branch of your issue tree, e.g., "We need to understand key aspects of the market such as how it's growing; because if it is shrinking, that would make it less profitable for the client long-term." Remember that you're trying to engage a CEO-level person with your structure, so don't ask them a bunch of questions as if they are a research firm to be delegated to, but instead share your hypotheses to engage them in problem-solving.

Now that you know what the interviewer is looking for, let's turn to what tools we can use to can create effective structures.

Section 3-2 Generic frameworks to memorize

There's a broader debate about whether interviewers want you to memorize frameworks for the case interview. I had colleagues and friends who succeeded in the case interview without memorizing frameworks. I, on the other hand, memorized frameworks when I went through the case interview process, so I see the merits of both sides of the argument and know that candidates on both sides succeed. However, I advocate that you memorize generic frameworks and apply them in the case interview because McKinsey recycles frameworks across multiple client engagements and advertises that it does so to its clients.

McKinsey's selling point is that instead of providing a client with just a single consulting team, it uses its global network to deliver the best of the firm to all clients. Here are a few quotes from McKinsey's values [8]:

- "(to) use our global network to deliver the best of the firm to all clients"
- "(to) follow the top-management approach"
- "(to) bring innovations in management practice to clients"

These points are achieved by recycling frameworks. In fact, McKinsey reviews its consultants to see if they are effective at translating parallel concepts across ideas and scenarios, bringing relevant knowledge and capabilities to clients, understanding and applying core functional/industry concepts, leveraging core knowledge in engagements, and capable of navigating the firm to access relevant knowledge and tools.

But there's a key distinction between regurgitating a pre-canned framework versus tailoring it to your client's specific problem. McKinsey also reviews whether its consultants apply frameworks and knowledge themes with adaptations to the client context. What this means on the case interview is that you need to cater any generic frameworks to the client's situation. What are your hypotheses for this client problem?

Another reason I advocate for memorization is that you only have 2 minutes max of silence to develop your framework and begin presenting it to your interviewer, so having some frameworks memorized and in your back pocket can be handy.

What frameworks should you memorize? There are 6 frameworks that are worth memorizing that I show in Figure 3-1 through Figure 3-6. I present these in order of priority. The first two frameworks—market entry and profitability—you will apply frequently, in at least 60% of the cases you do, such as for the Electro-Light [9] case on the McKinsey website. M&A cases (Figure 3-3) appear less frequently such as the Globa-Pharm [10] case on the McKinsey website.

The remaining three frameworks on aggressive revenue growth, pricing strategy, and operational improvements will come up even less, but you should prepare for them when they arise. In addition, prepare to pull these last 3 frameworks out to answer sub-questions within a case, e.g., brainstorming questions the interviewer may ask in a market-entry or profitability case about alternative revenue growth options, pricing strategy, or operational improvement opportunities.

Notice that in the figures below, I've spelled out example hypotheses under each point that you would present in order to engage the CEO and other functional leaders at the client. Be sure to adapt these hypotheses to your unique client situation. This way you show that you have thought through this client's problem rather than regurgitating a framework. It's this kind of hypothesis-driven presentation style that allows you to lead the most effective problem-solving session with the client and your team members, and it assures your interviewer that you are a hypothesis-driven problem-solver.

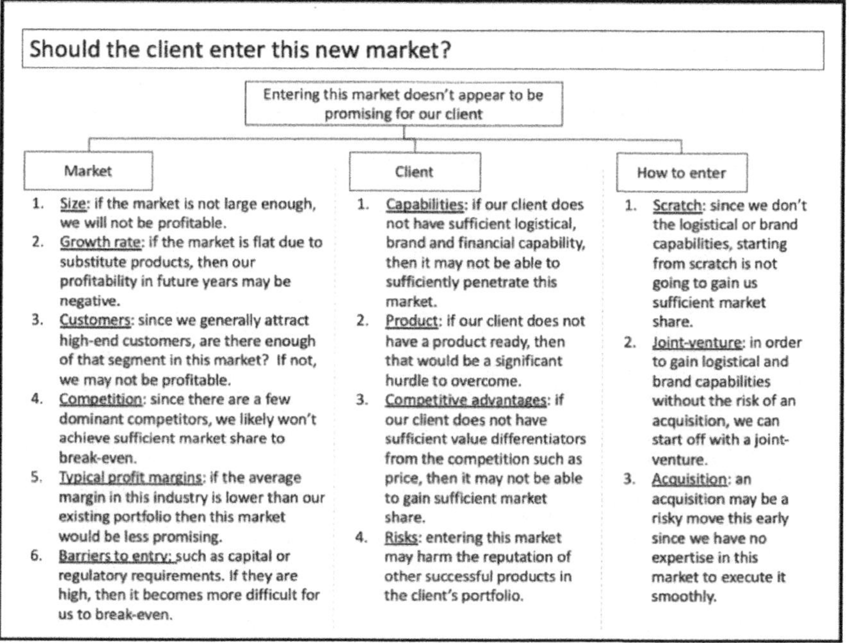

Figure 3-1 Market entry or new product generic framework. Use this framework for market entry problems or launching-a-new product problems. (Note that the hypothesis-driven language used is not generic, but should serve as an example that you adapt to the client problem).

For the market entry framework (which you can also use for new product problems), keep in mind that you also need to adapt your hypothesis-driven language based on the financial metric that is most important to the client. If the client is interested in revenue growth, then don't use the "break-even" and "profitable" language that I use in the generic framework. Instead, talk about how competitors will keep the client from reaching its revenue growth goal. This advice assumes that you obtained these financial goals in the "Define problem" step (Step 1) of the 7-Step Problem-Solving Process during the Clarifying Questions part of the case that we discussed in depth in Section 2-3.

Many of my case interview coaching clients present these concepts using high-level "Internal" and "External" buckets instead of the three high-level buckets I've used here. If Internal/External is something that you already use, that's a fine approach to continue using.

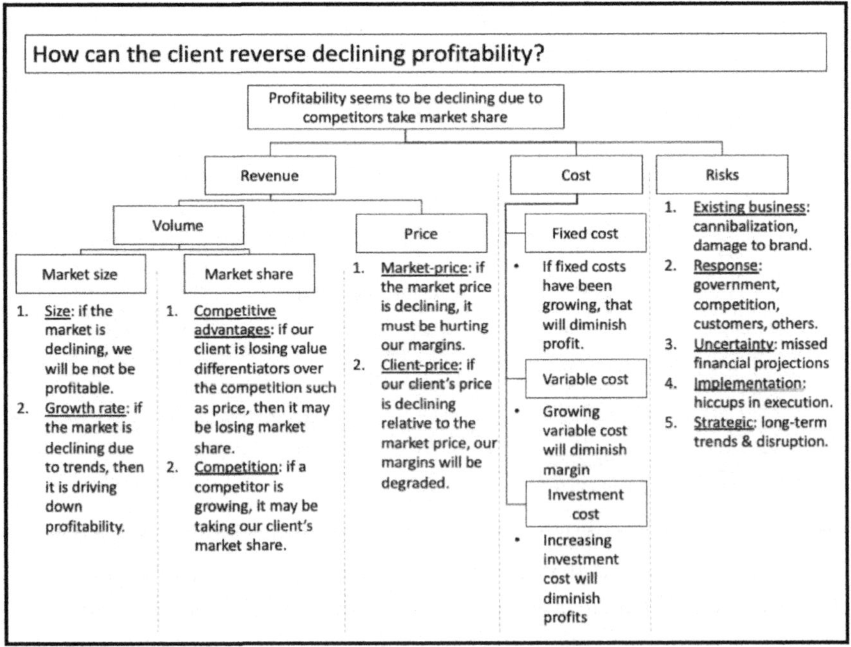

Figure 3-2 Profitability generic framework. You can use this generic framework for any client problems where a decision is being made based on maximizing profitability.

You can apply the profitability framework to any client problem where improving profitability is the goal, e.g., when profitability has been declining for an unknown reason, or when the client is assessing an opportunity or decision for whether it will improve overall company profitability.

Notice that the profitability framework explores many of the same qualitative concepts that are explored in the market entry framework, but under the revenue bucket such as market size, market growth, and competitive advantages. If it makes the memorization task more manageable for you, think about the profitability framework as a permutation of the market entry framework.

The "Risks" bucket in the profitability framework should be used to evaluate any initiatives that you will be recommending to the client. For example, if you plan to recommend that the client raise the price of one of its products in order to increase profitability, make sure you evaluate whether raising the price will result in cannibalization, competitor response, uncertainty, and so on.

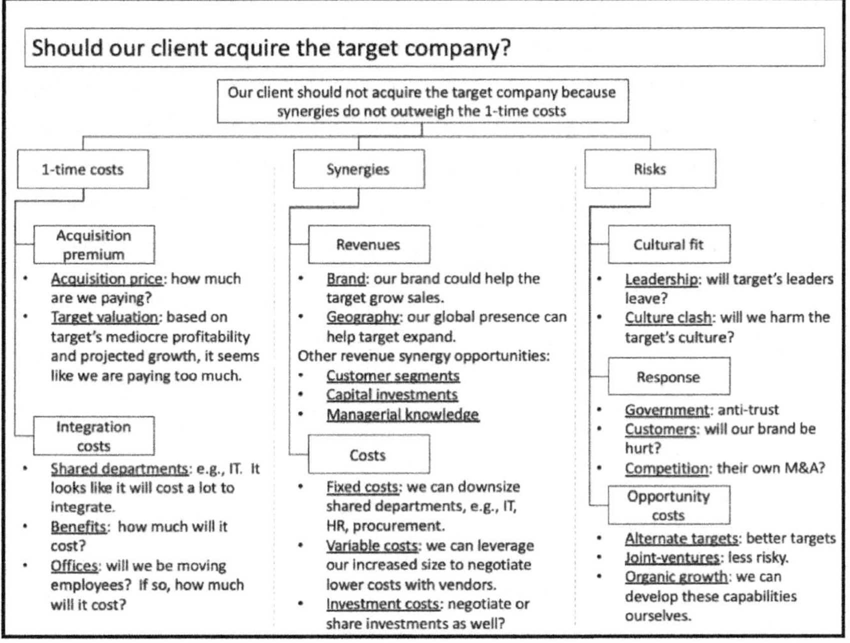

Figure 3-3 Mergers and acquisitions (M&A) generic framework.

You can understand the M&A framework as a cost-benefit analysis. The "1-time costs" and "Risks" buckets cover the costs; the "Synergies" bucket covers the benefits.

In addition, one advanced concept that you need to understand in order to grasp the M&A framework is that of the "Acquisition premium," which is the first sub-bucket under "1-time costs." When one company acquires another, the acquisition price that the two parties agree upon is almost always at a premium over the target company's market valuation. Otherwise, the target company's shareholders wouldn't agree to being bought out. The acquisition therefore only becomes worthwhile to the acquirer if it can gain back that premium through the synergies that will come out of the acquisition.

There are integration costs as well that the acquiring company will incur such as the work to integrate the IT systems, offices, health insurance plans, and so on for the two companies. And the acquiring company needs to gain back the cash lost to these integration costs through the synergies achieved as well. Otherwise, the acquisition deal will not be worthwhile.

Regarding the "Opportunity Cost" sub-bucket under "Risks": the acquisition isn't the best strategy for the client if there are better companies on the market for them to acquire; if they can achieve the same capabilities and synergies at lower cost and less risk through a joint-venture; or if they can develop these same capabilities and synergies organically from scratch with their own internal capabilities within their desired time frame and at lower cost.

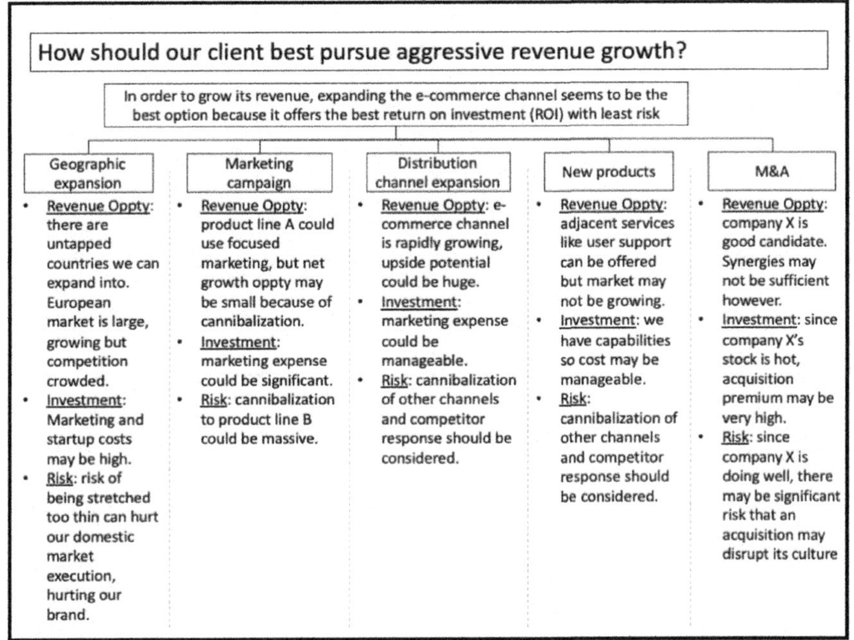

Figure 3-4 Aggressive revenue growth generic framework.

I based the aggressive revenue framework on the concept of return on investment (ROI), since all the growth options involve making an upfront investment to grow revenue. Which option gives you the best bang for the buck? Since investments always involve making a major change to the status quo, it is important to keep the risk of those disruptions in mind.

For the final two frameworks, if there is not an underlined title for bulleted text, that means that the bulleted text is an example hypothesis you need to adapt for your situation.

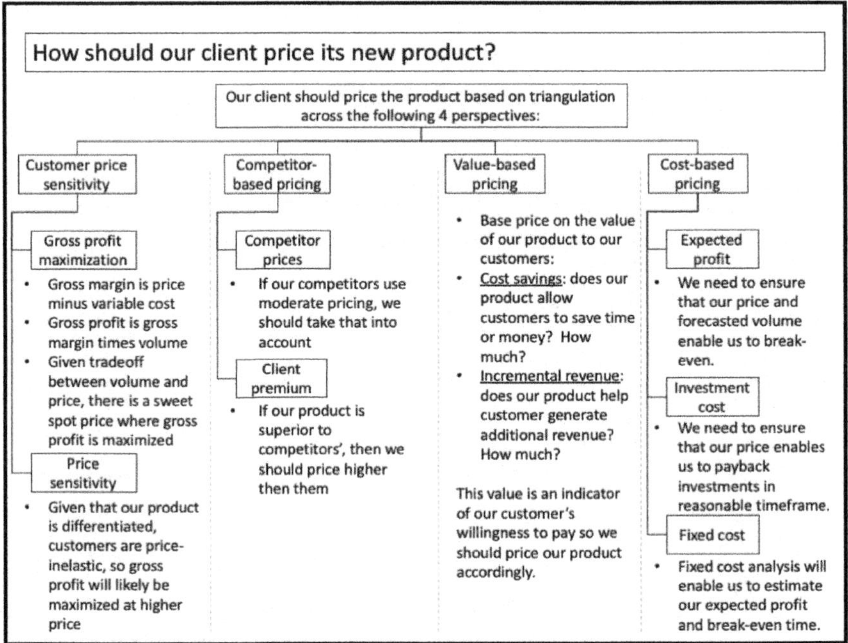

Figure 3-5 Pricing strategy generic framework.

Under the "Innovation" sub-bucket in the cost-cutting generic framework, for example, you need to test hypotheses for innovation in back-office functions (that could mean switching to a more automated payroll software or any ideas for innovative cost-cutting from other industries) and all other cost categories in the high-level list.

Memorizing frameworks can only get you so far as there are infinite kinds of potential client problems that a consultant can face, and therefore that you may face in the case interview. We now turn to strategies for developing your own customized frameworks for situations for which the 6 generic frameworks presented above are not appropriate.

Section 3-3 Creating customized structures

Often in the case interview, the interviewer will give you a question for which none of the 6 generic frameworks above is appropriate. In these cases, you

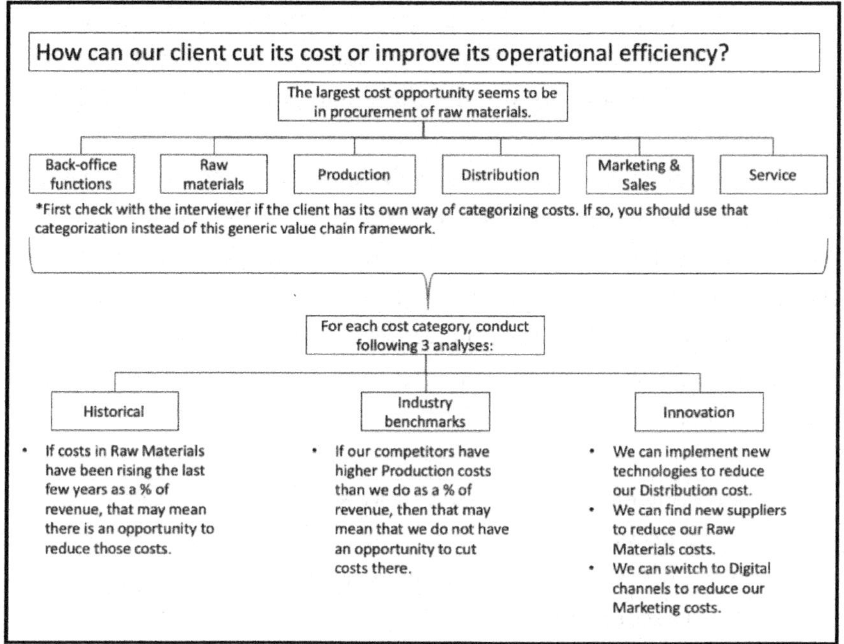

Figure 3-6 Cost-cutting or operational improvement generic framework.

need to create a custom structure on the spot. In addition, as we'll see in the next chapter on Conceptual Problem-Solving, the skill of being able to structure brainstorming questions can boost the volume and breadth of creative ideas you can brainstorm. Here I'll introduce to you 4 tools to keep in your Analytical Problem-Solving toolkit for creating customized structures.

I cannot stress enough, however, that all 4 of these tools require a robust problem definition. You need to make sure you do a thorough job at the Define Problem step (Step 1) of the 7-Step Problem-Solving Process coming into the structuring part of the case interview.

Custom-Structuring tool #1: Equation-based structuring

What metric is the client using to measure its success in working with us to solve this problem? Is it profitability, return-on-investment (ROI), net present value (NPV), unemployment rate, population growth, or cost-vs-benefit for example? Whatever that metric is, break it into its mathematical components and use those components as the buckets of your structure.

For instance, let's say the case is about whether we should invest in a new piece of machinery [11], and the client's objective is to decide based on NPV. First, make sure we're using the client's definition of NPV. Assume the interviewer responds that NPV is equal to present and future cash flows discounted for the time-value of money based on how far into the future the cash flow occurs. In that case, the high-level bucket structure could be:

1. Investment costs today to acquire and set up machine
2. Cash flows
    a. Profitability impact of the machine
    b. Discount rate
3. Lifespan of the machine.

These three components represent all the components needed to calculate NPV. Notice that we also included the lifespan of the machine because future cash flows cannot go on forever from this machine but only for the machine's lifetime. Under each point, we'd discuss hypotheses for estimating the value; e.g., for point 2, we'd discuss the increase in revenue and reduction in fixed and variable costs that the machine will create.

This equation-based approach allows you to get to the heart of the issue.

<u>Custom-Structuring tool #2: Multiple metrics of focus</u>

Sometimes the client is focused on multiple metrics. In that case, you can ensure that you are covering all the ground that you need to cover to give them the best solution by having one bucket for each metric.

For example, let's say that Google's Chrome Browser business unit has hired your consulting firm to help it develop a plan to increase user engagement and number of users of the Chrome browser. As in the previous example of the machine investment, let's make sure we understand the client's definition of these metrics. If you ask, the interviewer may tell you that Google defines user engagement as the percentage of users who use Chrome at least once a day, and number of users is how many people have Chrome installed. Then your structure could be:

1. Number of users
   a. Segment by region
   b. Segment by user device
   c. Segment by operating system
   d. For all three segmentations, look at:
      i. Marketing
      ii. Product features
      iii. Competitor browser used instead of Chrome and reasons for use
2. User engagement
   a. Users who open Chrome once a day
   b. Users who open Chrome once a week
   c. Users who open Chrome rarely or never
   d. For all three categories, look at:
      i. Marketing
      ii. Product features
      iii. Competitor browser used instead of Chrome and reasons for use

I defined the high-level buckets here based on the 2 metrics of importance to the Chrome business unit. The two lower level buckets (i.e., on customer segmentations and marketing vs product features and competition) is a structuring that I determined using the "Customized Levers" tool, which is the 3rd tool in this list that I'll turn to now.

Custom-Structuring tool #3: Customized "levers"

What are all the "levers" that we can pull to help the client improve the metric they are interested in? A lever is a simple machine such as a seesaw that you can use to move a heavy object. Here in a metaphorical sense, a lever therefore is an opportunity we can pursue to drive impact for the client. If the client has asked you how to improve profitability, the two levers available to you are revenue and cost.

In other cases, you must brainstorm what the complete set of levers available to you are. In the Google Chrome case, the levers I thought of for the second level structure would be users by region of the world, users by device such as mobile vs Mac vs PC vs tablet, and so on. The next level levers I thought about were all the different categories of reasons that someone chooses a browser based on: they've heard of its reputation (marketing), they like its features (product features), they selected a competitor for other reasons (competition).

Let's say the interviewer gives you a case about an energy company who is gauging how to manage the cost associated with its operations it has outsourced to a network of rural subtractors. Here, what are all the levers you can think of for reducing the costs? What comes to my mind are:

1. Re-negotiate existing rates with subcontractors
2. Find new subcontractors who will give us better rates
3. Help existing subtractors lower their costs
4. In-source and do the work of the subcontractors ourselves.

To use this method, you need to understand the key metric the client is interested in. Make sure you listen for any clues in the prompt of potential levers that interviewers will give you, and be innovative a little.

Custom-Structuring tool #4: Leveraging information in the prompt

Often the prompt will contain a list of items that can serve as your structure, such as a list of phases in a process, a set of events, or aspects of the problem that the client needs to take into account.

In the Google Chrome browser case, let's say that in a brainstorming question, the interviewer asks, "How can the Chrome team respond to the market share that Microsoft's Edge browser has taken?" Notice that the interviewer shared with you things that Microsoft did to take that market share: they launched a strong marketing campaign for Edge and made it more secure and more respectful of privacy, and they designed the Windows 7 operating system to restrict the browser that could be used. When you respond to the interviewer's question, you could have three buckets, one for each initiative of Microsoft's that the interviewer mentioned in the prompt.

Another example would be if the interviewer listed 6 steps in a manufacturing process in a case about operational improvement [11]. Those 6 steps could be your structure. (These instances where you are using a client's process as your structure are the sole exception where you can violate the rule of having 5 or fewer buckets in your structure as laid out in Section 3-1).

To show you how effective these 4 tools can be for creating custom structures, let's turn to some cases in an industry that can feel unfamiliar for interviewees and that always requires custom structures: non-profit cases.

Section 3-4 Structuring for public sector cases

Non-profit cases can be from the public sector, and they will always require a custom framework since the 6 generic frameworks presented earlier are relevant to for-profit business settings. Let's consider three example cases to show you how to apply the 4 tools presented in the prior section to any non-profit case.

<u>Non-profit case example #1: State Governor</u>: your client is the governor of a state. Before she is up for re-election, she wants to boost the state's population by 10% and bring unemployment down by 3 percentage points [12].

Here we need to apply Tools 1, 2, and 3. We should apply Tool 2 (multiple metrics) for the high-level structure. We should apply Tool 1 (equation-based structuring) for the second layer structure. And we should apply Tool 3 (customized levers) for the third layer structure.

Here is how I would do it:

- Unemployment rate
    - o # of people who can't find jobs
        - Incentivize new companies to come into the state to create jobs
        - Incentivize existing companies in the state to hire more
        - Train workers to be a fit for existing open positions
        - Create jobs through government funding
        - Stimulate the economy to grow
        - Develop resources to match job seekers with available jobs
    - o # of people in the workforce looking for work
        - Incentivize unskilled laborers who don't have necessary skills to leave the workforce to enter college or training programs
- Population
    - o Immigration (people moving into the state)
        - Market the state as a great place to live
        - Invest in programs that will make the state a better place to live, such as reducing the crime rate and creating shared institutions like libraries
    - o Emigration (people moving out of the state)
        - Research why people are leaving the state
    - o Birth rate
        - Offer couples tax incentives to have more children
        - Offer other programs to lessen the financial burden on families of having more children
    - o Death rate
        - Research ways to prolong the life of the average citizen in the state.

I have listed the two metrics the governor is striving to improve, broken them into their mathematical components, and then listed some levers to drive those components in the direction needed to get us closer to the governor's goals.

Non-profit case example #2: Coyotes: *Your client is the non-profit coyote preservation organization. They have enlisted your firm to help them develop strategies to stop the population decline of a near-extinct species of coyote in Coyote National Park [13].*

Here we can apply Tools 1 (for the top level) and 3 (for the second level):

i. Population growth
   - Immigration into the National Park
     - Are there other regions in the country or world where we can bring members of this species of coyotes from?
   - Emigration out of the National Park
     - Construct a fence to prevent escape
     - Research why coyotes have left in the past
   - Birth rate
     - How can we speed up coyotes' breeding? Can we induce the mating process?
   - Death rate
     - How can we prevent premature deaths of coyotes?
     - Are coyotes being hunted or dying of starvation?

You can be even more creative than me with thinking about all the levers we can pull to improve these metrics of death rate, birth rate and so on. Have fun with it.

Non-profit case example #3: Gates Foundation: *Your client is the Gates Foundation. It has asked you to develop a vaccine development strategy for the following year.*

Here I would first confirm the metric that the Gates Foundation uses to measure its success. Here the interviewer may say that it is the change in the number of people afflicted by disease from our vaccine work with the budget available. As discussed in the Define Problem step of the 7-Step Process, we'd also want to confirm what timeline the Gates Foundation has in mind. The interviewer may say they're considering a 5-year horizon when estimating the change in the number of people afflicted by disease.

Here I would think about what levers (Tool #3) we can pull within vaccine development to reduce the number of people afflicted by disease over the next 5 years. (Note that if you ask the interviewers about the Gates Foundation's project categories for vaccine development, they may give you a few thoughts, or the interviewer may have mentioned that in the prompt, which would enable you to use Tool #4).

1. Existing vaccine production
2. Existing vaccine distribution
3. New vaccine lab research
4. New vaccine clinical testing

For all 4 buckets, we'd want to dig into the following questions:

- What regions are experiencing a shortage of vaccines for a widespread disease?
- How much would it cost to have an impact?
- How long would it take to have an impact? e.g., research is an extensive process; can we develop a new vaccine and distribute it to people for impact within 5 years?
- Are there pharmaceutical partners we can work with to accomplish more within our budget?

Under the 4 levers, I've thought about the quantitative aspects of number of lives, time to results, and cost versus budget.

Now that we've covered how to create the structure, let's move on to the two critical steps for effective communication of your structure to your audience (the interviewer in the case interview, or the client CEO in a consulting engagement). These two steps—Prioritizing Issues and Planning Analysis—are important first, to engage your audience in hypothesis-driven problem-solving and second, to show the interviewer you are a hypothesis-driven problem solver.

Section 3-5 Prioritizing Issues (Step 3 of the 7-Step Problem-Solving Process)

One way to share your hypotheses with the interviewer is to prioritize the issues in your structure. If you take, for example, our structures for the State Governor and Coyote cases, it would be important to speak to your client about which branches we hypothesize to be the largest drivers of impact and which we don't think will be. I would suspect that the levers that the Governor can pull to drive the most impact before re-election are immigration and emigration (for population), and incentivizing new companies to come to the state and incentivizing existing companies to open new offices in the state (for unemployment rate).

It's sufficient to share a few thoughts about what you think are the most important buckets.

Section 3-6 Planning Analyses (Step 4 of the 7-Step Problem-Solving Process)

Planning analyses using hypothesis-driven language is the most important way for you to tailor your structure to the client, offer color and depth to your structure, and engage the client in problem-solving. Not offering sufficient depth is the number one mistake my coaching clients make during the upfront structuring phase of the case. As a result, <u>of all the sections in this chapter, please assign the greatest weight to this one.</u>

Your client is paying you to solve a specific problem for them, not to come in and ask them a bunch of questions. Therefore, when you present a structure, there needs to be a clear connection between every sub-branch that you present to the overarching client question. The client is thinking, 'how is this branch of analyses going to help me?' The senior partners on your team are thinking the same: 'how is this analysis going to help us deliver client impact?' You can make that connection clear by sharing your hypothesis for that sub-branch and implying how you might test that hypothesis (i.e., planning analysis to test that hypothesis).

So far, our hypothesis-driven approach has been in abstract language. Following is a full concrete example of the presentation I'd give to an interviewer (or client CEO) for my structure for a case.

Interviewer: Our client is a burger fast-food chain that is considering acquiring a donut chain of restaurants. The two companies have differing regional structures for managing their franchises. Our client is much larger than the donut company and has an international presence. However, the donut company is growing. Should they move forward with the acquisition? [11]

(Step 1: Define Problem)

Me: First, I'd like to make sure I'm defining the problem precisely. The objective is to make a recommendation to the client about whether they should acquire the donut chain. What financial metric is the client using to measure the success of this decision?

Interviewer: That's correct. The client measures success based on net present value (NPV) or long-term profitability.

Me: Is there a time-horizon or specific threshold target they have in mind for NPV or profitability?

Interviewer: No time-horizon. They are considering all future cash flows. The minimum profitability or NPV is net positive or greater than zero.

Me: Are there any hypotheses or initial rationale that client has for considering this acquisition?

Interviewer: No. The client would be open to any thoughts you had about how this acquisition could help the business.

(Step 2: Structure Problem)

Me: Can I have a moment to structure an approach for this problem?

Interviewer: Yes.

[I have 60-120 seconds to draw up a slide on a horizontally oriented sheet of blank printer paper that eventually resembles Figure 3-3.]

Me: Here is my structure on this slide. If the synergies that we can achieve once we integrate the donut company do not outweigh the one-time costs of the acquisition, then it would be a bad idea to move forward. As you can see here in my slide, I've broken my approach into 3 buckets:

1. *One-time costs: My first bucket is one-time costs.*
   a. *Acquisition premium:*
      i. *If we need to pay a hefty premium to acquire this donut company, we need to take that into account to see if we can pay that back.*
      ii. *If we think the donut company is over-valued, maybe because its management sacrificed profit margins in favor of its growth, we need to take that into account as an additional acquisition cost on top of the acquisition premium.*
   b. *Integration costs:*
      i. *How much will it cost us to integrate the donut company into ours once we acquire it? Because the two companies are both in fast food, we could integrate a lot of their regional management structures and food supply chains. But we need to account for the cost of doing so. The client could also integrate back-office functions like HR, IT, and corporate management, but we need to account for those integration costs.*
2. *Synergies: Moving on to my 2nd bucket, which is Synergies.*
   a. *Revenue synergies: First, I think there are several revenue synergy opportunities to explore and estimate. Can our brand help*

the donut company's brand? Since we are larger than them, can we use our international network to expand the donut company's geographical presence? Can we sell each other's products in each other's stores, such as donuts as a dessert or breakfast in the burger stores? Can we take some leadership talent in the donut company that is helping it grow and use them to help our burger business? We need to estimate these things.

   b. *Cost synergies: We can reduce costs based on the ideas I mentioned earlier when I discussed integration costs: sharing regional managerial structures across the two companies, and sharing back-office functions like HR, IT, and corporate management. How much will we be able to save in terms of offices that we can sell? Can we use increased size to better negotiate with suppliers for reduced food raw materials costs?*

3. *Risks: My third and final bucket is on Risks.*
   a. *Cultural fit: let's gauge the possibilities that the culture of one company can hurt the other. The donut company sounds like it is very entrepreneurial because it is growing fast and I'm concerned that we may damage that culture by acquiring it. Will the donut company leaders leave after the acquisition?*
   b. *Response: Will the government prevent the merger because of anti-trust? Will one company's brand hurt the other? I'm concerned that if we sell donuts in the burger store, it may damage our brand.*
   c. *Opportunity costs: I want to rule out that there aren't better opportunities out there for our client, like other acquisition targets that are more suitable; joint-venture opportunities, maybe even with the donut company; or if we can launch a donut product ourselves to accomplish the same without the risk associated with an acquisition.*

Interviewer: Great, thanks.

First, you can see that this presentation of the structure is wordy and at ~535 words. It would take me a little over 4 minutes to present. But the structure is the single most important part of the case, so it is worth showing the interviewer you are hypothesis-driven here. Also, by (1) showing the interviewer my slide and (2) presenting the entire high-level layer before going into the details of each bucket, she can interrupt and re-direct me between my buckets as she sees fit to manage the time. (Managing the time in the case interview in the interviewer's responsibility).

Second, notice how I've loaded this presentation with hypotheses, e.g., about potential synergies around selling each other's products in each other's stores, about the risks of acquiring a fast-growing company and killing its culture, about taking one company's geographical network to create opportunities for the other. This is the nature of the conversation you can have with a client CEO or a senior partner in your consulting firm to engage that person in problem-solving. I accomplished that by having a hypothesis for each sub-branch of the framework to serve the purpose of connecting that sub-branch to how we'll use it to answer the client's overarching question.

Third, notice how the hypotheses also serve the purpose of providing depth tailored to this specific client's problem and a plan for analyses. It's clear that we aren't regurgitating a framework—even though I applied the generic framework from earlier in the chapter to get to this structure—and it's clear what analyses we will do, e.g., appraise the likelihood that the donut company leaders will depart after the acquisition in the "Risks" bucket.

You may have noticed in this chapter that quantitative concepts formed the backbone for many of the structuring problems we worked through. Also, the skill of Analytical Problem Solving reinforces the other two problem-solving skills, the first of which we turn to now.

CHAPTER 4

Conceptual Problem Solving

"It's really hard to design products by focus groups. A lot of times, people don't know what they want until you show it to them."–Steve Jobs, 1998 interview in BusinessWeek [14]

This Steve Jobs quote demonstrates that analytical problem solving on its own cannot deliver brilliant solutions. You need to add some thinking outside the box or creativity. Creativity or brainstorming is one part of conceptual problem-solving. Conceptual problem-solving is the skill of developing creative qualitative solutions and insights, sometimes from conceptual thought in a vacuum, but also from driving insights out of quantitative data such as exhibits.

Section 4-1 How interviewers test your conceptual problem-solving skill

The case interview tests conceptual problem-solving in three ways:

(1) your ability to understand the client's business model and two types of questions that appear later in the case than the initial structure:

(2) brainstorming questions
(3) exhibit interpretation

In the interviewee-led format, if your structure touches on the important areas for investigation, your interviewer will ask you to brainstorm thoughts in an area of your exhibit or provide you with an exhibit, putting you into a situation equivalent to that of the interviewer-led scenario.

Your ability to understand the client's business model is what some may consider a skill that comes from business intuition or the ability to understand qualitative business concepts. Interviewers are looking to see if you can apply general business concepts in the case interview to drive insights to help the client.

When interviewers ask you conceptual problem-solving questions, they're testing to see if you can develop creative solutions and insights. With brainstorming questions, interviewers want to see if you can be innovative for the client rather than sticking only with the first cookie-cutter answer that comes to your mind. My rule of thumb for brainstorming questions is that you need to provide at least 7 non-overlapping ideas. For exhibit interpretation questions, they're looking to see if you can make astute observations, but also whether you can plan creative hypotheses that the data support or creative opportunities to address issues arising from the data.

I've structured the rest of this chapter based on the 3 ways that the case interview probes conceptual problem-solving.

Section 4-2 Client Business Model

As I mentioned in Section 2-3 on the Clarifying Questions part of the case, when you're at the Clarifying Questions stage, your goals include defining the problem (Step 1 of the 7-Step Problem-Solving Process). In addition, you need to use the Clarifying Questions portion to understand the client's business model. Many of my case interview coaching clients have found the acronym "VOM" useful to ensure they are asking the appropriate questions to achieve these two goals during Clarifying Questions. The VOM acronym is:

1. **V**alue-chain: the sequence of businesses who serve some role to contribute to creating a product/service that a consumer enjoys.
2. **O**bjective: the goal. This is covered by the "Define Problem" step that is the first step of the 7-Step Problem-Solving Process. I described how you can accomplish effective objective-setting and defining problems in significant detail in Section 2-3, so I will not spend any more time on that topic in this chapter.
3. **M**oney: how the client makes money, i.e., the client's revenue streams.

Value Chain

A common mistake on the case interview is taking for granted that our client is a B2C (business-to-consumer) business; when many businesses are B2B (business-to-business), meaning that their customers are other institutions. Be careful about the distinction between a "consumer" and a "customer." A consumer is an individual human being who enjoys a product or service. Whereas a customer is a more general term that could be an individual or an institution that purchases your client's product or service.

Whether your client is B2B or B2C has huge implications for your structure and your approach. For example, if your client is a pharmaceutical company, your strategy would be very different if the company sold prescription versus over-the-counter medications. In the former, your customers would be a small group of physicians, pharmacies, and insurance companies who get the drug into the hands of consumers. In the latter, you are selling to consumers who look for your medication on the shelves at pharmacies.

Therefore, the first aspects of your client's business concept that you need to nail down during the Clarifying Questions are where do they sit in the value chain and what value do they create in that value chain? Who are their customers? Businesses or consumers? If they are businesses, what types of businesses? An energy distribution company, for example, would have as its customers utility companies, and it transports energy for those utility companies using an infrastructure of power lines. That's important to know and apply during other parts of solving the case.

Money

You need to make sure you understand your client's revenue streams. If your client is a soccer team, what are all its revenue streams? Jersey sales, TV rights, ticket sales, and so on. If your client is a company like Google that offers its products free, how does it generate revenue? The revenue streams will often be clear in the initial prompt, but sometimes they are not clear, so you need to ask.

Basic ("stupid") background questions

I concede that this category of questioning is not in the VOM acronym, but it's just as critical. If there is any concept that isn't clear to you, you need to understand it before you create your structure. Sometimes we're shy about asking these basic background questions, so just concede that maybe you're asking a "stupid" question and do it anyway.

This is important for B2B cases where you have no personal experience being a customer of that business. For example, if your client manufacturers a drug that treats stroke and you do not know about stroke treatment, make sure you ask the interviewer how patients receive it, how often they take it, how they learn about it, and so on. If patients play no role in selecting their treatment because the drug is prescription, you need to be aware of that so you focus marketing efforts on doctors, not patients. In my final round interview with McKinsey, one of my interviewers gave me a case about oil production, and although I was embarrassed, I asked the interviewer what does it mean to "produce" oil? He began his response by saying that it was a good question, and I did well on that case.

If you make it a point to understand these three areas during the clarifying questions, you'll have a solid understanding of the client's business model.

Section 4-3 Brainstorming questions

We began the discussion of how to handle brainstorming questions in Section 2-5. Here let's go deeper into each of the three steps laid out in that section:

Step 1: Define the problem: Pull out a new slide (i.e., a blank sheet of paper that you orient horizontally) and write the objective at the top of your slide. If there is any opportunity for ambiguity or lack of clarity in the interviewer's question, make sure you iron it out with them.

Step 2: Structure the Problem: Develop a structure to come up with the broadest, most thorough set of brainstormed solutions. Structured brainstorming was important for me because as an engineer by training, I wasn't someone with inherent business intuition or creativity, and I found that being able to brainstorm the maximum number of ideas for every bucket in my structure led me to come up with a greater volume and broader set of creative ideas.

It's acceptable to request some time to create your structure. But don't request or take over 30 seconds of silence for questions other than the initial structure. Since you've already taken up to 2 minutes of silence for the upfront structuring, the interviewer can't afford to give you too much time for every question. Sometimes, the interviewer will need to decline your request for time because they are running up against the time slot allotted for the interview.

There are 4 paths you can take to creating your structure:

i. *Perspective of a stakeholder*: is it useful to see this situation from another stakeholder's perspective? For example, if the question is about how we can an gain market share, let's define the structure based on how a customer chooses their product from multiple competitor selections: (a) price, (b) quality, (c) channel convenience, (d) brand reputation, (e) referrals. Then we can populate each of these 5 buckets with ideas to improve in those areas to gain market share. Even if we come up with just 2 ideas under each bucket, that's 10 ideas right there, which is well beyond my 7-idea minimum threshold.

ii. *Leverage ideas from your upfront structure*: Often you can recycle buckets from your upfront structure. For example, in the Coyote case from Section 3-4, if the interviewer asked me a brainstorming question about what might cause the Coyote population to decline, I would use my upfront structure as is and brainstorm ideas under each sub-bucket. Many of my case interview coaching clients forget that this is an option, but it is an easy opportunity, so make it a point to take advantage of this opportunity whenever you can.

iii. *Use one of your generic structures*: if in the middle of a case about launching a new product, the interviewer asks you for ideas about how to determine the price of the new product, you can pull out the structure for pricing strategy from Figure 3-5 (assuming you have it memorized).

iv. *Custom-structuring tools*: If the prior three points aren't applicable, use one of the custom-structuring tools in your toolkit we discussed in Section 3-3. If, for example, the question is to brainstorm a list of ways to increase profits, use the equation-based structuring tool to create a typical profitability structure for your brainstorming.

Once you've created your structure, it's time to do the actual brainstorming.

<u>Step 3: Prioritize issues</u>: Here you share your hypothesis of where you think the most value will come from.

<u>Step 4: Plan analysis (partially)</u>: This is where you brainstorm a list of ideas under each bucket of your structure. (This corresponds with the "Plan Analysis" step of the 7-Step Problem-Solving Process because in

the broader client engagement, you are coming up with ideas you plan to further investigate to make the best recommendation to the client).

Here you should not be as methodical, and instead let loose and brainstorm off-the-wall creative ideas. Try to be unfiltered so you don't suppress your creativity. You can always prioritize your ideas afterwards if you want to make it clear to the interviewer which of your ideas you think are unlikely to fly or are impractical.

Step through your buckets from your structure one at a time from left to right, and brainstorm as many ideas as possible under that bucket before moving on to the next one. My rule of thumb here is that you want to get at least 7 non-overlapping ideas. If you can brainstorm over 7, that's even better. The best-case scenario is that the interviewer cuts you off to tell you that you've brainstormed enough and that it's time to move on.

Here are four approaches that have helped me brainstorm a volume of quality ideas:

i. *Ideas from the same industry*: the first and most basic set of ideas comes from learning from (or copying) the best-in-class competitors in the same industry as your client. In the state governor case, what can our governor learn from what other states are doing to attract companies?
ii. *Parallel concepts from other industries*: this is where you can have the most fun. What have you been seeing in the news that companies in other industries do that we can apply? For example, Amazon's search for its second headquarters (HQ2 project) [15] offers a lot of lessons for the state governor to attract new companies.
iii. *Applications of general economics and business concepts*: apply basic concepts that you've come across in Econ 101 or from your practice cases such as supply and demand impact, leveraging economies of scale, customer price sensitivity, or the BCG growth-share matrix [16].
iv. *Human aspect*: never forget the human aspect when it comes time to be creative. Empathize. Will certain stakeholders get

upset? Will certain customers be affected and react? What about employees in the company?

These are approaches that interviewers would appreciate because consulting firms review their consultants in one respect for their ability to look across their firm as well as outside of it for additional inspiration, examples, and ideas that can help their current client. The ability to find and learn from analogous cases is important.

Let's now put it all together and walk through a brainstorming example from start to finish. For this example, let's assume we're in the middle of a case interview about an airline.

Interviewer: To increase profitability, the client is considering re-deploying the aircraft used for its service from Mexico City to Bogota, Colombia, to instead use it to increase the frequency of its Mexico City to Los Angeles flight. What are the risks associated with making this move?

Me: Okay, so we are brainstorming risks associated with eliminating the Bogota route and adding frequency to the Los Angeles route. Do you mind if I take 30 seconds to develop a structure for brainstorming ideas?

Interviewer: Why don't you just talk me through what you're thinking instead?

Me: Sure. I'm laying out on my slide here (see Figure 4-1), *a simple profitability structure that we can use to think through the distinct risks: I have "Revenues" and "Costs." I'll break "Revenues" further into "Volume" and "Price." And I'll break "Cost" into "Fixed," "Variable," and "Investment."*

Under "Volume," I'll first think about the risks to our volumes from eliminating the Bogota flights. It may hurt our brand image in Colombia which could affect the sales of our other flights in the region. Competitors in Latin America may portray this move of ours as opportunistic in their marketing. There's the risk that the Bogota market may grow in the coming years, which we'd be missing out on.

Next I'll think about the risks of adding frequency to the Los Angeles route. We will cannibalize the sales of our existing flights between Los Angeles and Mexico City. Our competitors in the US may respond by adding to their Los Angeles flight frequency or by launching a marketing campaign to diminish our success. The already strained relationship between the United States and Mexican governments could further deteriorate, which would hurt our sales for this route.

Under the "Price" bucket, I don't see any risks from eliminating the Bogota route. But by adding to the frequency of the Los Angeles route, we increase supply and therefore could cause the market price for that route to go down, hurting our revenues. Competitors may also start a price war with us to get us out of the Los Angeles market.

Moving on to "Costs" now, under "Fixed costs," one risk of eliminating the Bogota flight is that we may end up incurring significant marketing costs to manage the damage to our brand in Latin America. When adding frequency to the Los Angeles route, we may end up spending more on marketing than expected to launch the new flights.

Under "Variable costs," there are not any risks from eliminating the Bogota route, but for adding to the frequency of the Los Angeles route, fuel charges may be much higher in Los Angeles than in Bogota. Under "Investment costs," there isn't any risk from eliminating the Bogota flight, but when we add frequency to the LA flight, the existing aircraft may require major renovations and upgrades to comply with different regulations in the United States.

Interviewer: Good list, thanks.

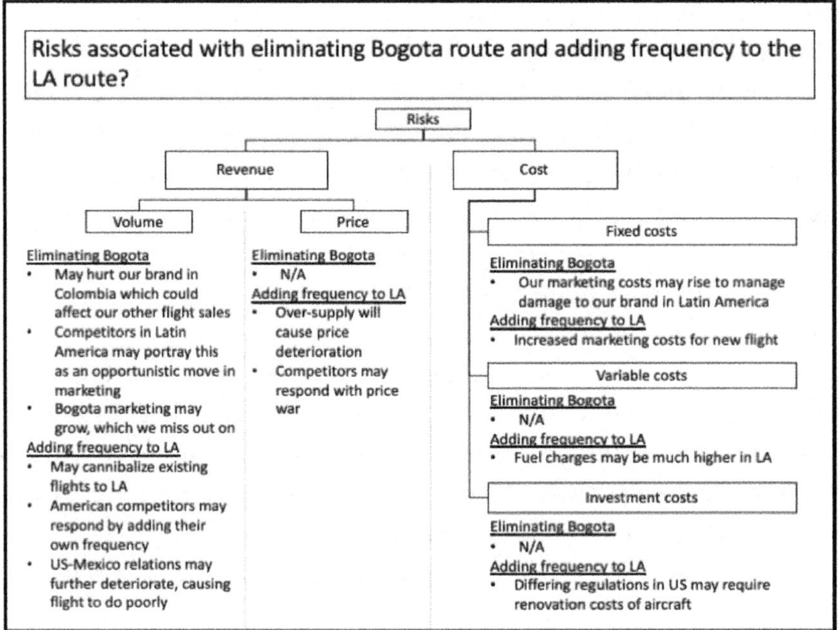

Figure 4-1 Brainstorming example. Slide that I'd draw up in response to interviewer's question about risks associated with airline's decision to eliminate the Bogota to Mexico City route to redeploy aircraft to increase the frequency of the Los Angeles to Mexico City route.

By using structured brainstorming, I could come up with 12 ideas, well over the minimum threshold that I recommend of 7. I used the profitability structure here because that was the metric of most concern to this client. Let's move on now to the last category of questions that interviewers use to test your conceptual problem-solving skill.

Section 4-4 Exhibit interpretation

We began our discussion of how to go about responding to exhibit interpretation questions in Section 2-6. Here let's walk through an example from start to finish to show how to apply each of the 7 Steps of the Problem-Solving Process when the interviewer slides an exhibit in front of you.

Let's go back to the M&A case that we introduced in Section 3-6 where our client was a burger chain that was weighing whether to acquire a donut chain.

Interviewer: Here's an exhibit that the client's finance department put together for us. (Interviewer slides a piece of paper towards me). *Based on this data, what synergies do you think might be available?*

	Client (burger chain)	Target (donut chain)
Stores		
Total	5,345	1,116
North America	3,742	1,094
Europe	1,069	22
Asia	428	0
Other	107	0
Annual growth in stores	11%	14%
Financials		
Total store sales ($,MM)	$5,691	$689
Parent company revenues ($,MM)	$1,935	$209
Key expenses (% of sales)		
Cost of sales	54%	39%
Restaurant operating costs	22%	27%
Restaurant property & equipment costs	4.80%	8.30%
Corporate general & administrative costs	7%	16%
Profit as a % of sales	6.33%	4.98%
Sales per store ($,MM)	$1.06	$0.62
Industry average ($,MM)	$0.92	$0.79

Table 4-1 Exhibit for case about client burger chain looking to acquire a donut chain.

(Step 1: Define Problem)

Me: Okay, so our objective here is to identify synergies between the two companies. Are we interested in both revenue and cost synergies, or just cost synergies?

Interviewer: Both.

Me: Okay. Can you clarify for me how the client defines what a synergy is?

Interviewer: Great question. A synergy is a benefit that can be captured beyond the sum of the two individual companies on paper.

(Step 2: Structure Problem)

Me: Okay. Here on my slide (see Figure 4-2), *I will keep track of both revenue and cost synergies. I will also structure based on the rows in this exhibit: "Stores," "Financials," "Profits," and "Sales per store."*

(Step 3: Prioritize issues)

We'd expect at least some cost opportunities to be present in a typical acquisition. However, it's the revenue opportunities that can determine whether these two companies are a suitable fit for each other. So, revenue opportunities are the higher priority.

(Step 4: Plan analyses)

Can I take about 30 seconds to look over this table to make sure I understand it?

Interviewer: Sure, take your time.

(30-second pause)

(Step 5: Conduct analysis)

Me: Starting with the "Stores" section of the exhibit, I can see that on the "Revenue" side, the Client has more stores than the Target, so the Client can sell the Target's donuts in its stores to achieve a revenue synergy. Next, the Client has a strong international presence in Europe and Asia, whereas the Target has miniscule presence in those continents. So, the Client can use its capabilities in those continents to help the Target grow there. I can see that the Target has a faster growth rate than the Client, so the Client can adopt some growth strategies from the Target.

Moving on to "Costs" in the "Stores" part of the exhibit, because the Client has a much larger footprint in terms of stores, the two companies can together negotiate lower costs for supplies they need for their buildings like cash registers, cleaning supplies, tables, chairs, and so on. Next, the Client can use its capabilities to lower the costs for the Target to expand into international geographies. The two companies can also save on marketing costs by sharing their marketing efforts.

Moving on to the "Financials" section of the exhibit, I can see that the Client has an order of magnitude more store sales than the Target, so even more reason to believe that the Target can leverage the Client's brand to sell more of its donuts. For cost opportunities, I can see that the Target has a lower cost as a percentage of sales, so its management can share those cost-efficiency strategies with our Client. The two companies can negotiate better raw materials costs from farmers and food vendors through economies of scale. The Target also has higher operating costs than the Client, so the Target might learn from the Client how to lower that. The two companies can both lower their sales, general and administrative, and property, plant, and equipment costs by sharing those resources.

Under "Profits," the Client has a higher profit margin than the Target. The economies of scale discussed earlier can help the Target match the Client's profit margins. And in the "Sales per Store" section, the Client is doing well relative to its industry average in sales per store, whereas the Target is lagging its industry average. The Target can learn strategies from the Client to increase its sales per store.

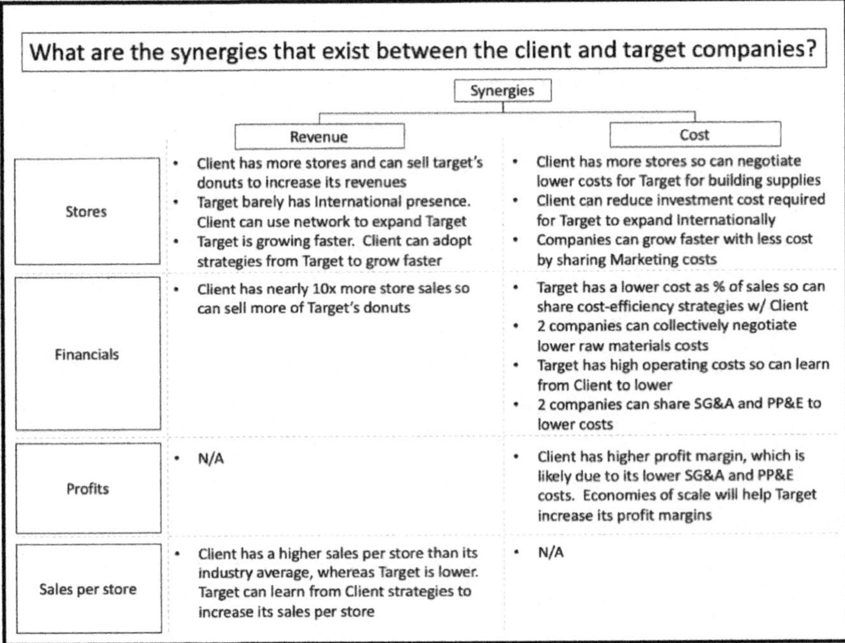

Figure 4-2 Exhibit interpretation. The slide (i.e., notes) that I would draw up to walk my interviewer through my interpretation of the exhibit in Table 4-1.

(Step 6: Synthesize analysis)

Overall, taking inventory of these opportunities on the Revenue side, I see promising opportunities for our client to turbo-charge the Target's business.

(Step 7: Develop Recommendation)

As next steps, I'd want to confirm that selling donuts in the burger stores and that expanding the Target's donut business overseas would succeed—for example is there appeal for American donuts in Asia and Europe? If the answer to both questions is yes, I'd want to size those revenue opportunities for the client.

Interviewer: Okay that sounds like a plan.

You can see that asking a few clarifying questions off the bat to define the problem helped me create my eventual structure of "Revenues" and "Costs." I also structured using the sections of the exhibit so I made sure to spend time on each one to extract as many insights as possible. It is vital to follow through on the 6th and 7th steps of the Problem-Solving Process at the end to show the interviewer you are a proactive thought leader who drives to the next steps.

Let's now turn to the final problem-solving chapter.

CHAPTER 5

Quantitative Problem-Solving

"All models are wrong, but some are useful."–George E. P. Box, British Statistician, 1919-2013 [17]

Although George E. P. Box was a statistician, this quote is even more applicable to the quantitative modeling that consultants carry out. That's shown by one of the most used phrases in McKinsey jargon that I came across in my time there: "SWAG", meaning a **S**ophisticated (or Scientific) **W**ild-**A**ss **G**uess.

Since I was coming from an engineering background, I wasn't used to making such rough approximations as made in building business models. As a result, I avoided numbers altogether, and I was slow to quantify my findings for my consulting clients. That was a mistake because the value that management consultants bring is being data-driven and scientific in order to influence clients. And although the model may be "wrong" (i.e., not 100% accurate), providing an educated and scientific approximation is still "useful" as George E. P. Box pointed out.

Although I was hesitant to quantify things because of the "wild-ass guess" part of making SWAG's, someone coming from a non-quantitative background may hesitate to quantify things because of the "scientific" part of making SWAG's. Whatever your reason for worrying about the math on the case interview, I want you—in the spirit of George E. P. Box—to dive into the math with confidence because either way you'll be wrong, but quantification is the most compelling way consultants communicate ideas to clients.

Section 5-1 How interviewers test your quantitative problem-solving skill

The case interview tests your quantitative problem solving using specific questions where you're requested to calculate something. Those questions could involve an exhibit that the interviewer gives you, or it could involve data that the interviewer provides you with. In the interviewee-led format, you may have to first identify the opportunity to calculate a quantity on your own that the interviewer would then confirm. If you don't, the interviewer will take notice that you did not suggest a calculation and guide you in that direction.

However, even in the interviewer-led format, it's your job to plan the method and ask for any additional data that you need for the calculation. Therefore, in either format, you will need to connect the dots to determine what is possible to calculate and how.

When they test your quantitative problem-solving skill, interviewers are looking to see not only how good at math you are, but whether are you able to plan the overall approach. For example, the notorious market-sizing questions aren't difficult because of the math required, but because of the open-endedness, ambiguity, and data sources involved in developing the approach.

Regarding math errors and accuracy of your calculations, don't fret too much about never making a math error. In my experience, you can make up to 2 minor math errors (i.e., thinking 10 plus 20 is 40 after you've already proven you can do much more complex math leading up to that error) per interview and still score high on math. Interviewers will give you that benefit of the doubt, however, only if you communicate your process at each step so that they can follow along with you without having to spend excessive mental energy.

However, if you make any kind of error early in your analysis without giving your interviewer the opportunity to catch it (through clarity of communication), then you create frustration for them to have to troubleshoot your math after you've arrived at the wrong answer. That frustration is something they do not want to deal with on a real client engagement, which would be a sufficient reason to not extend you an offer.

The best way to accomplish these goals of developing an approach for quantitative analysis, carrying out effective math, carrying out accurate math, and doing so in a manner easy for the interviewer to follow is to adhere to the 7-Step Problem-Solving Process with an emphasis on communicating your work.

Section 5-2 Define Problem (Step 1)

A frequent mistake that my case interview coaching clients make in the case interview is answering the wrong question. For example, calculating pay-back period of an investment in number of years when the question was for them to calculate the valuation of an investment. Or calculating revenue and stopping, when the question was for them to calculate profits.

Put bluntly, get the "Define Problem" step right. What are you being asked to calculate and in what units? If it's market size, is the interviewer asking for the market size in customers or dollars? Write the objective and its units at the top of your slide (i.e., your horizontally-oriented blank sheet of paper) and put a box around it.

In the example above about being asked to calculate the valuation of an investment, it would be worthwhile to ask the interviewer how they define "valuation." Is there a specific mathematical definition that the client wants us to use? The problem of glossing over mathematical definitions is one I see with questions involving unemployment rates. Interviewees will often assume that unemployment rate is the total people looking for work divided by the population instead of the number of people in the labor force. Always ask the interviewer what definition they want you to use, as part of the "Define Problem" step of the Problem-Solving Process.

If you're someone who hesitates to do math, then be wary of asking too many clarifying questions. Interviewees who hesitate about math burn a lot of time by asking too many clarifying questions when they should have moved on to structuring the math much more quickly.

Section 5-3 Structure Problem (Step 2)

A frequent mistake on the case interview is to respond to a math question by jumping straight into doing computations: "I will assume the population of the United States is 300 million," or jumping straight into asking the interviewer for random pieces of data. The problem with doing that is your approach might not be the best one. It's more efficient to present a high-level approach to your interviewer (or the client and the senior partner in a real consulting engagement) and get their feedback before going down the wrong rabbit hole. If you ask for random data without first providing a structure, it may come across as stalling because you don't know how to develop an overall approach to calculate the metric.

So how do you structure the math? There are three approaches that are robust enough that you can use one or some combination for most questions.

<u>Math structuring approach #1: Current-state vs Future-state</u>

This is the most powerful of the three approaches. We can frame most math problems as a comparison between the current-state and some hypothetical future-state. In this structure you'd have two columns: one for the current-state and one for the future-state. And you'd have a series of rows for the relevant metrics involved that you need to compare across the two states.

Here is a sampling of a few example quantitative analyses that the current-state vs future-state framework can address:

- Decision facing the client (or comparing multiple options on the table): what is the impact on client profitability of pursuing a certain decision? Lay out the relevant financial metrics for the current-state in one column and for the potential future-state in another column. Then compare across the two to see which has a greater profitability.

- Impact of a change: if one parameter in a system changes, such as the water level in a dam, and you need to calculate what impact that has on hydro-electric energy production. You can calculate the current-state of hydro-electric energy production in one column and the future-state of hydro-electric energy production given the reduced water level in the dam in the second column.
- Changes needed to get to a desired state: let's say that the state governor wants to bring down unemployment from 8% to 5%. How many jobs does she need to create? Do the math for the current-state in the first column and repeat those steps in the second column for the future-state so you can compare across the two columns the number of jobs required.

Let's now consider an example math question where we could apply this structure. In this example, the interviewer presents a case where the client is a manufacturer of jets for government defense departments [18]. The client is trying to determine where to build its next manufacturing plant among three options: the US, Argentina, or Italy. Given that this is a decision facing the client, we could use the "Current-state vs Future-state" tailored to be a 3-column math table: Option 1 vs Option 2 vs Option 3, or US vs Argentina vs Italy as the location of the new manufacturing plant.

Figure 5-1 shows how my slide would look as I walked the interviewer through my structure and calculation. (At the structuring step of the interview, however, you would not have filled any numbers into the table, and you might not have labeled many of the rows).

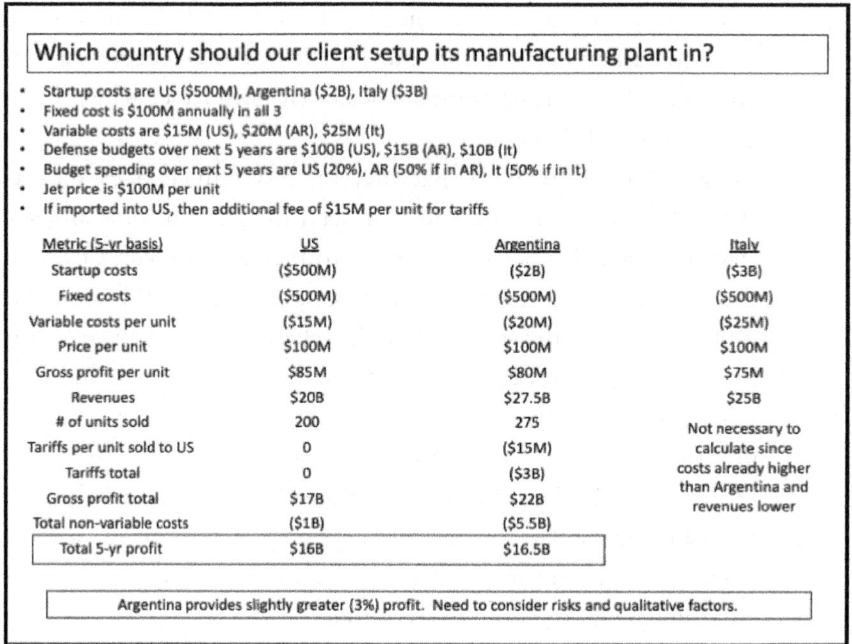

Which country should our client setup its manufacturing plant in?

- Startup costs are US ($500M), Argentina ($2B), Italy ($3B)
- Fixed cost is $100M annually in all 3
- Variable costs are $15M (US), $20M (AR), $25M (It)
- Defense budgets over next 5 years are $100B (US), $15B (AR), $10B (It)
- Budget spending over next 5 years are US (20%), AR (50% if in AR), It (50% if in It)
- Jet price is $100M per unit
- If imported into US, then additional fee of $15M per unit for tariffs

Metric (5-yr basis)	US	Argentina	Italy
Startup costs	($500M)	($2B)	($3B)
Fixed costs	($500M)	($500M)	($500M)
Variable costs per unit	($15M)	($20M)	($25M)
Price per unit	$100M	$100M	$100M
Gross profit per unit	$85M	$80M	$75M
Revenues	$20B	$27.5B	$25B
# of units sold	200	275	Not necessary to calculate since costs already higher than Argentina and revenues lower
Tariffs per unit sold to US	0	($15M)	
Tariffs total	0	($3B)	
Gross profit total	$17B	$22B	
Total non-variable costs	($1B)	($5.5B)	
Total 5-yr profit	$16B	$16.5B	

Argentina provides slightly greater (3%) profit. Need to consider risks and qualitative factors.

Figure 5-1 Jet manufacturer case, math question response. Example of the "Current-state vs Future-state" structure.

What I would do is explain to the interview that I'd use these three columns, one for each potential plant location, to walk through a comparison of the three locations for a series of metrics that I'd lay out as the rows of the table. I'd also explain that I'd arrive at a row at the bottom of the slide to represent total profitability or cash flow that I'd used to compare each of the three potential country locations as the basis for providing a final recommendation. I'd then wait to see what feedback the interviewer had before I dove into working with real numbers.

<u>Math structuring approach #2: Market-sizing using chronological buckets of analysis</u>

Sometimes, the interviewer will ask you to forecast the client's revenue or profit when entering a new market, launching a new product, doing a market-sizing. You can treat these forecasting exercises similar to market-sizing questions because there's not a current state to compare to, and you must plan a method to obtain needed data from the interviewer (or in a real consulting engagement, what data you need to pay for). For these math questions, you need to lay out a chronological set of buckets that represent phases of analysis that you need to conduct.

Here is a generalized version of a market-sizing framework to forecast profits:

1) Revenue forecast: first, let's estimate revenue, which I will model as market size times our client's market share.
   a) Market size estimation
      i) Customer population by segment. Segment in the most appropriate way, e.g., by age, by disease profile, by gender, size of institution, etc. How you segment requires some creativity and hypothesis-driven thought. If it's a case about a niche product like Iranian movies, segment by nationality, not by age. How many customers are in each segment?
      ii) Penetration percentage estimation by customer segment. This is a critical piece. You need to test any assumptions you make:
         - What percentage of customers will choose a substitute instead? For example, surgery instead of the client's medication.
         - What percentage of customers can afford the product?
         - What percentage of customers want the product but choose not to buy it for other reasons?
         - Are there additional assumptions, like what percentage of insurance companies will reimburse for the drug?
      iii) Aggregate customers: Multiply customer segments by penetration percentage and sum up to get total customers.
      iv) Average revenue per customer. Determine this based on the price per unit times the number of units purchased per year by an average customer.

v) Total market size: Multiply the total customers from (iii) by the average revenue per customer from (iv)

b) Market share estimation. Make an educated guess of what market share our client will get based on the criteria that customers use to select a brand of product and how we compare to the competitors in those categories:

i) Competitors

ii) Customer decision criteria

- Brand reputation
- Price
- Quality
- Convenience of doing business with
- Others factors...

iii) Client's product offering: how it compares to competitors' in customer criteria

c) Revenue forecast: Multiplying market size estimate times market share forecast will give revenue forecast

2) Cost forecast: Now that we've forecasted revenue, we need to forecast or estimate costs to obtain profitability.

a) Fixed cost forecast: brainstorm the fixed costs associated with this business and estimate the cost of each.

b) Variable cost forecast: what are the raw materials and processing involved in production and how much will they cost?

c) Investment cost forecast: are there upfront costs that we need to account for?

3) Profit forecast: Forecasted revenue from Step (1) minus forecasted costs from Step (2) will give the forecasted profits.

The steps I placed in bold-face font are those where interviewees often forget critical considerations and that you should pay closest attention to. If the interviewer only asks you to forecast revenues, you need not walk through steps on costs.

Keep in mind that the starting point of your analysis can also vary depending on the context. If, for example, this is a case about a disease, often you can start with the population of patients living with that disease that your team can find in medical journals, instead of having to segment yourself.

The key point I want you to understand here is that you are the thought leader and therefore you have to propose the method. Then the interviewer (or client or senior partner on your team) will engage with you in problem-solving and provide you with feedback. Never start off by saying, "What data do we have?" Because in a real consulting engagement, it is the consultant's job to propose a method and the sources of data to pull from. The client can offer suggestions building on your proposal, but it's your job to be the thought leader.

Let's now consider a concrete example. Your client is a pharmaceutical company that has developed a new drug for treating heart attacks [19]. Let's say that after you and the interviewer finish walking through your upfront structure, the interviewer asks you to forecast the revenue in year 1. Figure 5-2 shows how I would go about structuring the math. I

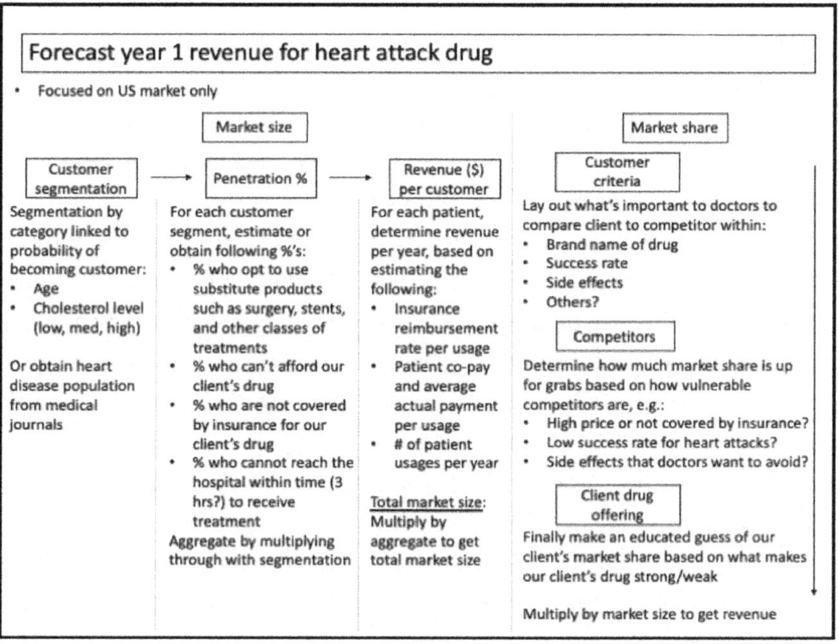

Figure 5-2 Structuring the calculation for the heart attack drug revenue forecast question using the market-sizing approach.

would walk my interviewer through this slide and then wait for her feedback to see if I should change the approach.

I chose not to use a full profitability example because the steps to estimate cost are more straightforward. Pay close attention to my structure for the heart attack drug revenue forecast. Notice how I made sure not to gloss over any significant assumptions, such as making sure we take into account what percentage of people with a heart attack can make it to the hospital in time. Furthermore, maybe only a fraction (e.g., 10% of the population in the medical journal paper) who have a heart attack will ever choose to get treated because the rest have silent (i.e., unnoticed) symptoms? These are the kinds of things that as a consultant you need to ask about to arrive at the most "useful" mathematical model that you can create for your client.

Math structuring approach #3: Timeline

Some complicated math questions on the case interview are based on modeling events that happen at distinct points in time. But if you can draw out a clear timeline on your slide, you can keep the numbers and time-points straight to arrive at an accurate answer.

What I've seen happen is that the calculation may require you to multiply some quantity—it could be a time or financial quantity—by a factor of 2 to account for the need to do a round-trip. But many interviewees forget to multiply by a factor of 2 because they are preoccupied by the many other calculations that they need to do. That's a red flag to an interviewer because it implies that maybe you aren't the most organized person and you'll make careless mistakes that they'll have to constantly quality-check when you join their team.

You can avoid these kinds of careless errors by laying out on your slide a timeline structure. Walk through all the events that need to happen from start to finish ("from cradle to grave," as one of my McKinsey partners would say) for the process in question. Label each one of those events on your timeline if it has implications for your calculation. This way, you won't miss critical high-level concepts that you need to account for such as round trips. That structure then serves as the guideline for your calculation.

Let's now walk through an example. Your client is a wine manufacturer that needs your help to determine whether it should manufacture Merlot or Bordeaux [20]. The two wines have different yields per kilogram of grapes, different price-points per liter of wine, and different profit margins. To further complicate the situation, we have to store the two wines for different periods of time before we can sell them for revenue: Merlot has to be stored for 6 years whereas Bordeaux has to be stored for 12 years. Assume that the discount rate is 12%, and therefore that it takes 6 years for an investment to double in value based on the rule of 72 [21].

Figure 5-3 shows how I would structure the calculation for this question. There are two parts to the calculation: the first is to calculate the annual profits, and the second is to account for the time-value of money.

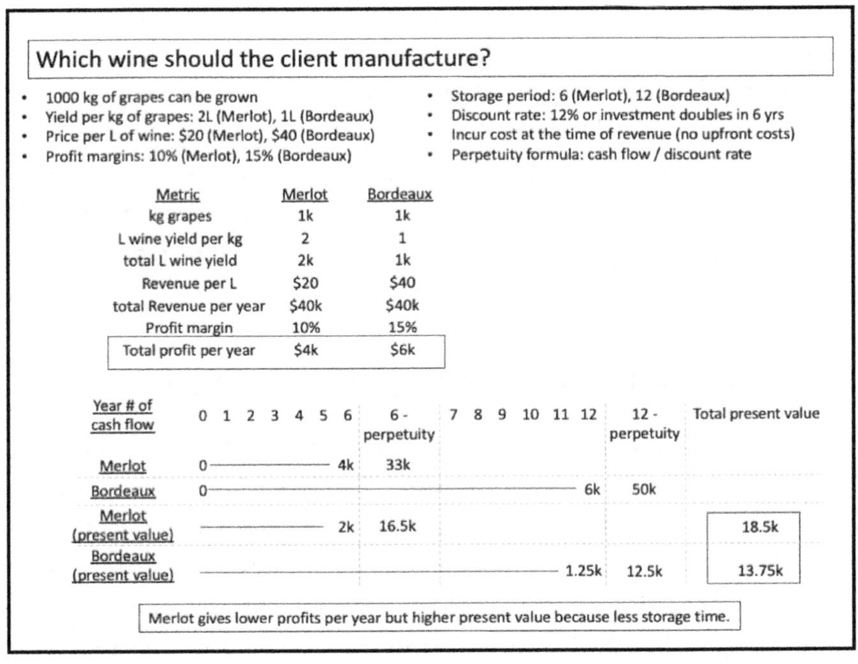

Metric	Merlot	Bordeaux
kg grapes	1k	1k
L wine yield per kg	2	1
total L wine yield	2k	1k
Revenue per L	$20	$40
total Revenue per year	$40k	$40k
Profit margin	10%	15%
Total profit per year	$4k	$6k

Year # of cash flow	0 1 2 3 4 5 6	6 - perpetuity	7 8 9 10 11 12	12 - perpetuity	Total present value
Merlot	0 —— 4k	33k			
Bordeaux	0 ——		—— 6k	50k	
Merlot (present value)	—— 2k	16.5k			18.5k
Bordeaux (present value)	——		—— 1.25k	12.5k	13.75k

Figure 5-3 Wine case, math question response. Example of the Timeline structure.

For the first part, I use the "Current state vs Future state" structure to compare Merlot to Bordeaux.

For the second part, I use a Timeline structure where each column represents a year. Because we can sell the aged wine for a profit every year in perpetuity, we need to use the perpetuity formula that the interviewer can give you, and that I have in the notes at the top of the slide. I'll walk you through the details of the calculation when we reach the "Conduct Analyses" step (Section 5-6).

How to structure when the calculation involves an interviewer-provided table

Many math questions will be based on a table that the interviewer slides in front of you. If you're not prepared for it, that can confuse you about which of these three structuring approaches to use. All three structuring approaches still apply, and you can use one or a combination of them just as you would if there were no table involved.

What should be different about your approach is that you may use the structure of the table (for example the table may already be in a "Current state vs Future state" format). Trying to create the structure from scratch may be less efficient than expanding on the structure that the table is already in. Maybe you just need to add a column to the table for your calculated quantity.

Section 5-4 Prioritize Issues (Step 3)

Now that you've laid out your structure, share a hypothesis about where you expect the most value to come from and therefore where we'd want to be more mindful of the analysis. For example, for the heart attack drug structure shared earlier (Figure 5-2), I'd mention after I laid out my structure that I'd expect the heart attack market to be a large but crowded one because of its maturity. Therefore, I'd expect the market size to come out to a huge number, but I think we need to spend much more time thinking through what market share we can realistically capture in such a competitive market.

Section 5-5 Plan Analyses (Step 4)

Calculation efficiency

When you plan how you'll calculate the metric, make sure you're being as efficient as possible. For example, if the interviewer has provided you financial data for the client on a per week basis, is it necessary to do the extra work to convert it into an annual basis? Maybe it's unnecessary because the principal goal is to decide between 2 options and comparing them on a weekly basis won't change the decision. Always ask yourself if you're calculating things that aren't necessary.

Also ask yourself if you're asking for data that isn't necessary. If the interviewer told you the revenue and the profit margin, do you need to ask for cost? You don't because you can calculate the cost from those pieces of data that the interviewer already gave you. (If the concept of profit margin is foreign to you, it's fine to ask the interviewer to define it for you, but also make it a point to look up terms as you encounter them during the preparation process).

Data sources

In the Plan Analyses step, you also need to share a sampling of where we can get the data needed and what mathematical analyses (e.g., multiplication, etc.) that we plan to do to get to the conclusive answer. It's most natural to talk through this while you're presenting each bucket of your structure. For example, in the heart attack drug case, I'd mention I would get the customer segmentation and segment size from medical journals. Under the customer criteria bucket, I'd mention that I may interview customers.

Other data sources that you can mention using are interviewing leaders or employees at the client, experts around the world, publicly available documents (such as on the SEC website) or public databases. Don't belabor how you'll conduct analyses, however. Just like we discussed in Section 3-6 about the planning analyses step for the upfront structure, keep your description of your plans for analyses brief while sharing plans for each sub-bucket of your structure.

One thing you should never do however is state that you'll "assume" a certain value for a certain number. The way you make a SWAG or sophisticated/scientific wild-ass guess is that it has to be scientific and therefore, supported by data. Have data or a rationale behind every number you use. Try to catch yourself whenever you use the word "assume." Say that you'll plan to interview a medical expert like a cardiologist to determine a reasonable number to use instead of assuming anything about heart attacks.

Section 5-6 Conduct Analyses (Step 5)

Now we are ready for the actual calculations.

Tables

It's important that you walk the interviewer through your calculations using a table (as in Figure 5-1 and Figure 5-3). That way, if you make any errors during an intermediate step of the calculation, it gets communicated to the interviewer while they're following your tabular structure and they can fix your error before it propagates through your entire calculation. Catching errors early in this way makes it less frustrating for both you and your interviewer. The oral communication that you'll use to walk your interviewer through your table as you do your math is something we'll discuss more in Section 7-5.

Getting into the habit of using tables for calculations is difficult for engineers because they're accustomed to writing equations in linear form in programming languages. I faced this struggle as well when I prepared for the case interview. But consultants and people in the business world use Microsoft Excel and think in terms of tables. Analysts, investors and CEOs are accustomed to seeing income statements and balance sheets as tables and they prefer to see the full tables because they need to know the intermediate breakdown of numbers.

Mental math is over-rated

Because catching errors is an energy-intensive and frustrating task for interviewers, it's more important that you minimize the errors you make in the case interview. One way to do that is to **forego doing mental math** in favor of carrying out math on a scratch paper. It only takes a few extra seconds, and interviewers don't mind waiting.

I use a scratch sheet of paper for all computations (see Figure 5-4 for an example) including computations as simple as multiplying a two-digit number by a one-digit number. It's very difficult to not make any errors at all, and if using a scratch sheet of paper can reduce the number of errors you make, then I'm all for it.

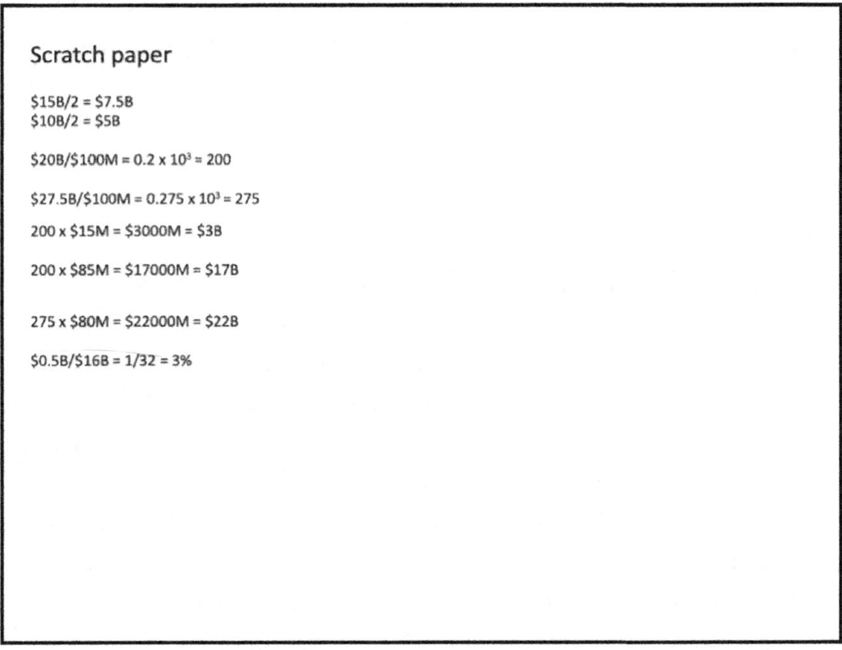

Figure 5-4 Scratch paper used for the jet manufacturer case to carry out the computations to develop the table in Figure 5-1.

Rounding

Rounding your numbers is okay as long as it doesn't introduce more than a 10% change or error in the final number. One exception to this rule is if you are doing a market-sizing estimation or any kind of educated guess (i.e., making a SWAG) about a number where you know that your estimate is a very rough estimate, anyway. In that case, it is okay to round as long as it doesn't introduce more than a 25% change in your answer. The other exception is if your interviewer tells you not to round.

I'm often asked if you should ask your interviewer for her permission to round a number. My preference that you do not ask for permission because it is your role to take thought leadership and make a decision whether a certain rounding step is going to introduce sufficient error into your analysis that it may change the recommendation or conclusion. Therefore, you should instead use the 10% or 25% suggestions in the prior paragraph, explain your rationale, and wait to see if your interviewer provides feedback.

Dimensional analysis

It's possible that I'm a big fan of dimensional analysis (an analytical tool used by chemists) because I come from a physical sciences background, but I still urge you to try it out. On my scratch paper, I would confirm that the mathematical operations or formula that I am applying are correct and make sense by seeing if the units cancel out so that the remaining unit is the correct one for my final answer.

Here's an example. Your client owns a burrito cart [19], and we need to forecast what the market size will be in the new food cart cluster where he is considering moving his cart. The food cart cluster is open 5 days per week, 4 weeks per month. On those days, the carts are open from 11:30am to 1:30pm. We measured that 100 customers per hour visit the cluster. The average amount a customer spends is $5. Here is how I would incorporate dimensional analysis into my calculation to make sure I am calculating correctly:

$$\frac{\$}{\text{month}} = \left(\frac{5\ \cancel{\text{days}}}{1\ \cancel{\text{week}}}\right)\left(\frac{4\ \cancel{\text{weeks}}}{1\ \text{month}}\right)\left(\frac{2\ \cancel{\text{hrs}}}{1\ \cancel{\text{day}}}\right)\left(\frac{100\ \cancel{\text{cust}}}{1\ \cancel{\text{hr}}}\right)\left(\frac{\$5}{1\ \cancel{\text{cust}}}\right) = \frac{\$20\text{k}}{\text{month}}$$

I laid out what I thought the formula should be to calculate the market size and made sure that I included the units for every number. I then found pairs where a unit appeared in the numerator in one spot and the denominator in another spot. In those cases, I struck out both in the pair since they cancel each other out. After repeating that for all units, I found that the two remaining units were "$" in the numerator and "month" in the denominator, which is the unit of the answer the interviewer asked for.

If I find that the resulting remaining units after canceling pairs does not match what the interviewer asked for, it's a sign that something in your formula may be wrong. This method requires that you lay out the units beyond what's normal. For example, if you just put "$5" in the last factor instead of "$5/customer" like I did, then it won't work out.

Sanity check math

One of the most frequent mistakes I come across in the case interview is interviewees finishing their calculation and then asking "is that right?" Consultants can't ask their clients if what they did was right, so you shouldn't ask your interviewer either. Instead, you could tell the interviewer you want to do a sanity check or see if your answer makes sense. Then take a step back and ask yourself some questions to quality-check your answer.

For example, does the order of magnitude of the answer make sense? If the task is to estimate the market size for a drug across the US, you'd expect the answer to be in the billions of dollars. If your answer is in the thousands, something isn't right.

You can also revisit all the steps you took to get to the answer and see if they all make sense and seem accurate to you.

Wine example

I want to return to the example of the wine manufacturer trying to decide between Merlot and Bordeaux because the math can be confusing. I'll continue where I left off in Section 5-3 walking through my slide in Figure 5-3.

For the first part of the calculation, when I created my structure, I did so by laying out a table to show the interviewer how I was using the "Current state vs Future state" structure. I continued to use that table for the calculations. I labeled the first few rows based on the quantities or metrics that I'd received data for from the interviewer: kg of grapes and liters of wine yielded per kg of grapes. I then started laying out rows for quantities I knew I needed to calculate next, like the total liters of wine yielded from the grapes. I repeated this process to list the revenue per liter (or price), total revenue per year, the profit margin, and the total profit. On my scratch paper, I would have done dimensional analysis to make sure the formulas I was using made sense from a units perspective, and to do the actual computations like the multiplications.

The second part of the calculation is more confusing. Merlot will generate a consistent cash flow of $4,000 every year starting in year 6 and beyond. So I first record the cash flow of $4,000 in year 6, and then a perpetuity of $33K (which I got by dividing $4k by the 0.12 discount rate). That $33K is the value of the perpetuity in the year before it begins, so I add a column called "6-perpetuity" to keep track of it. After repeating those steps for Bordeaux, I added two rows to determine the present value of those cash flows at various years that I recorded. I discounted those cash flows using the fact that a cash flow 6 years later is worth only half as much today, since an investment doubles every 6 years. After summing them up, we determine the total present value for both types of wine.

For the second part, it was critical that I listened to the interviewer and recorded how long the aging was for both wines, the perpetuity formula, the discount rate, and so on. You can see how I recorded everything at the top of the slide as the interviewer laid it out for me.

Section 5-7 Synthesize Findings (Step 6)

We've just finished the calculation and sanity checked our answer. Many interviewees think their work is now done. But the most critical steps of the process remain: translating your numbers into what it means for your client and continuing to drive to the final recommendation.

To "Synthesize Findings" (Step 6), tie your calculated number back to the context. Was it about choosing between two wines? If so, what do your calculated numbers say about which wine is better?

Be sure to tie in other pieces of information and considerations, and notice how when you combine that with your calculated numbers, it changes the synthesized view. For example, in the calculation for the jet manufacturer in Figure 5-1, we find that building the plant in Argentina provides 3% greater profits over 5 years than building it in the US. When we consider the geopolitical and other risks of building it in Argentina, maybe 3% is negligible and we may want to stay with the US.

Section 5-8 Develop Recommendation (Step 7)

Now that we've synthesized the findings of our math calculation, we either need to make a recommendation or lay out the next steps we need to take to make a recommendation. Unless the interviewer tells you it's time to meet the client and summarize your findings, you want to use that additional time to do more analysis, so lay out next steps.

For the wine example, even though the math shows that Merlot has a higher present value than Bordeaux, it would be worthwhile to confirm the following before making the ultimate decision to manufacture Merlot instead of Bordeaux:

- Customers: Is there sufficient demand for Merlot? Will it sell?
- Hybrid option: Is it possible to use half the land for Merlot and half for Bordeaux? Diversification could have its benefits.
- Capabilities: Is the staff trained in manufacturing either wine?

Lay these things out to the interviewer to show that you are a thought leader who will drive to making the best overall recommendation to the client.

We've now completed our discussion of Problem Solving. Now in Part II, we'll discuss what specific habits you need to emphasize to be an effective problem-solver in the case interview. Then in Part III, I'll lay out how you should best use your time to improve your problem-solving skills.

PART II

Habits of Communication

CHAPTER 6

Slide-making

"Much of our reporting relied on McKinsey's own words, memorialized in a medium the firm has mastered: the PowerPoint slide."– The New York Times, 2019 [22]

The opening quote for this chapter is one that applies for any management consulting firm. As a consultant, your product for your client is a PowerPoint deck, so any management consulting firm will have mastered the medium of the PowerPoint slide. If making slides is such an important part of being a consultant, and if you are planning to bring paper and a pen with you to your case interview to write with, then why not go ahead and further show to your interviewer you are a good fit to be a consultant by presenting your notes to them as slides?

Section 6-1 Why slide-making is important

Presenting slides to the interviewer does show that you'd be a good consultant, yet it's the least important reason that for me to dedicate an entire chapter to it in this book. The more important reasons are:

Reason #1: Enhanced problem-solving

The primary reason that I advocate for you to organize and present your notes to the interviewer as slides is that it serves you as a problem-solving tool, that enhances your problem solving. Slide-making allows you to organize your thoughts and your communications. Consulting is based on bringing organizational tools like structuring to large, messy problems. So by creating organized slides, you bolster that process.

For me, making slides with my pen and paper during the case interview improved my performance in the following ways:

- Math error reduction. By being able to organize in a table the many data points that my interviewer was throwing at me and the many intermediate quantities that I was calculating, I was better able to keep track of those pieces to walk through complex calculations.
- Final recommendation and synthesis efficiency.
    - By having organized slides for each analysis I did over the course of a case interview, when it came time for the proverbial elevator ride with the CEO, I could draw from my conclusions and analyses over the case to deliver a recommendation.
    - After finishing a math or brainstorming problem, I could look back on prior steps of the case to connect the dots and synthesize across those different data-points to update where I stood regarding an overall recommendation.
- Brainstorming volume. By organizing my brainstorming in a structured manner (the structured brainstorming that we discussed in Section 4-3), I could come up with a greater volume of ideas.
- Organized thought. I know that I used to be frantic and nervous during the case interview. That changed after I started designing my notes as slides. Slowing things down and being clean and organized in your note-taking can do wonders for your ability to be a thought-leader, and taking the time to create slides forces you to

do that. It's much like walking up to a white board and drawing things out for your colleagues as you lead them through a discussion. It organizes the thinking.

- Clarity of the final objective. When I got into the habit of writing the objective of a calculation or the overall case objective at the top of my slide, it kept me focused on driving the calculation forward until I answered the original question instead of forgetting the question and calculating the wrong thing.

Reason #2: Enhanced communication

The second reason I advocate for slide-making is that it is a powerful communication tool with the interviewer. If you have 4 buckets in your structure, and you show your interviewer a slide as you present, it ensures that they don't miss any of your important points while not having to take notes themselves. In addition, if they feel you are taking too long to present your structure, they can look at the other buckets on your slide and re-direct you to talk about another bucket in your structure that they are more interested in.

When you walk through a math calculation, if you have a clean table that shows your interviewer in an organized fashion the intermediate values in your calculation, it is much easier for them to catch any errors you make, which can save both of you frustration later on in the calculation.

One criterion that McKinsey uses to appraise consultants' performance as thought leaders is by asking whether this person is willing to step up to the white board and inclusively lead portions of problem-solving sessions. As a result, by laying out your thinking understandably on your sheet of paper and showing it to the interviewer in a manner that includes them in your thinking, you demonstrate that you are someone who meets a criterion of being a good consultant.

When you finish your interview, the interviewer will have to confiscate your notes to protect the confidentiality of the content. But they'll also refer to your notes when they complete their interview feedback and need to jog their memory of what insights you came up with.

Section 6-2 General guidelines for slide-making

There are few general guidelines for slide-making that I want to enumerate for you here:

- Landscape mode: PowerPoint slides are in landscape mode, so rotate your sheet of paper so it is horizontal (wider than it is tall). You'll notice that the slides I've shown in the chapters on Analytical, Conceptual, and Quantitative problem-solving all have the same aspect ratio as an 11" x 8.5" sheet of paper.
- 1 Slide per question: for every question, pull out a fresh sheet of paper and start a new slide. Consultants use one slide per idea. You need to use a separate slide for each part of the case or question.
- Abbreviations: because of the limited time you have in the case interview, use abbreviations. This is where the slides I've shown you in earlier chapters are not exemplary; I chose not to abbreviate words because I cannot walk you through my slide. For example, it's common to use the " symbol in place of "profit." You can define your own abbreviations as well such as 'R' instead of "Revenue," "Cust" instead of "Customers" and so on.
- Boxed title of the slide should be the objective of the question. As I explained earlier in this chapter and in our review of Quantitative Problem Solving, write the objective of the question at the top of your slide.
- Clear structure. There should be some clear structure on the slide, whether that's an issue tree for structuring or brainstorming questions or a table for math questions.
- Present the slide. As much as possible, show your slide to your interviewer. If you're presenting a structure that you've already jotted down, pick up the paper and show it that way. If you're writing out the slide as you talk through a math calculation, turn the paper in such a way that your interviewer can see it while you continue to write on it.

Let's move on to specific guidelines for slide-making for each type of problem-solving.

Section 6-3 Slide-making for Analytical questions

The slides you make for analytical questions are the slides for the upfront structuring part of the case. Use the figures in Chapter 3 as examples of what those slides should look like. You will, however, have to use abbreviations and will have much less time to write as much as I've written in those example slides.

But otherwise, as you look at the slides, notice the following aspects of the slides:

- clear issue-tree used to delineate buckets in the structure
- sub-bullets under each bucket
- title of the slide that reflects the overarching question of the case.

Regarding how much you need to write under each sub-bullet, that depends on how much text you need to remind yourself of what hypotheses you want to share with the interviewer in your oral presentation when you walk them through the slide. For example, whenever I deliver a presentation, including the presentations of my upfront structure in the case interview, I need bulleted notes for all the points I want to make so I don't forget them.

Look back at the example oral presentation of my structure outlined in the dialogue in Section 3-6. To give that level of depth in your presentation of your structure, think about how many notes you'll need on your slide. In addition, you need to balance how much you need to write based on how much you can get written on your paper in the 1-2 minutes that you have to come up with your structure before the interviewer wants to hear from you.

Section 6-4 Slide-making for Conceptual questions

For Conceptual questions, such as brainstorming questions and exhibit interpretation, use the slides shown in the figures in Chapter 4. For brainstorming and exhibit interpretation questions, to structure your brainstorming, you could use an issue tree format (Figure 4-1) or you could use a table (Figure 4-2). In these two slides, notice that the title of the slide is the sub-question for that specific brainstorming question.

For exhibit interpretation questions, the approach you take to slide making depends on whether you can write on the exhibit. If your interview is over video-conferencing or the phone, you cannot write on the exhibit. In some in-person interviews, the interviewer may prefer that you not write on their hard copy of the exhibit, and sometimes the interviewer is okay with you writing on their hard copy.

If you can write on the exhibit, I encourage you to take advantage of that opportunity if the exhibit provides some structure. If the exhibit is a table with rows and columns, you can use those rows or columns as your structure, step through each one and write your observations using that structure for each row or column. However, if the exhibit is a graph that does not have rows and columns, you may create your own structure on your own sheet of paper.

If you cannot write on the exhibit, pull out your own sheet of paper and create a slide as you would for a brainstorming question: title the slide, create your structure, and list observations from the exhibit under each bucket of your structure (see Figure 4-2 for an example).

Section 6-5 Slide-making for Quantitative questions

For math questions, use the figures in Chapter 5 as examples to mimic. One key rule for any math question is that you should not have any scratch work such as computations (e.g., multiplication signs, division signs) on your slides. You should do those computations on a separate scratch piece of paper such as Figure 5-4. It is okay to list out background information about the math question as the interviewer reads that out to you at the top of the slide as I have for all the math slides (except the scratch paper slide) in Chapter 5.

One of the prime reasons I use a scratch paper is because it makes the calculation less stressful for me. I feel that I have to fit less onto my slide, and I have more space to do all the scratch work that I need to do. It also minimizes the clutter on your slide that your interviewer needs to filter out when they are trying to follow your logic.

For questions for which you need to use a market-sizing type of structure, you must present an issue tree structure first, such as in Figure 5-2 before moving on to the math. For the two other structure types (i.e., "Current-state vs Future-state" and "Timeline"), you can communicate your structure using a table instead of an issue-tree (see Figure 5-1 and Figure 5-3).

Whenever you walk through your calculation using a table, make sure that the quantities you calculate at each intermediate step have some physical meaning. For example, you'll notice that every row in Figure 5-1 and Figure 5-3 has some physical meaning such as liters of wine yielded per kg of grapes. That way, both you and your interviewer can follow the calculation or troubleshoot it based on sanity checking each intermediate quantity, e.g., does it make sense that 1 kg of grapes yields 2 liters of wine? What I'm advising you against doing, for example, is taking the profit margin and multiplying that by the kg of grapes as an intermediate step before going on to the next step because that quantity has no physical meaning.

Since math questions have a final answer (unlike brainstorming or structuring questions), be sure to put a box around your final answer so you can find it later in the interview if the proverbial CEO asks you for a final recommendation on the spot.

A comment about note taking: I want to stress that taking sufficient notes when the interviewer shares information with you in the case background, question prompt or elsewhere, can be valuable. Often there are clues buried in that background information that can help you with your math and upfront structuring. Maybe the interviewer mentioned a key customer segment. Or there's an opportunity to use the "Leveraging information in the prompt" structuring tool that I described in Section 3-3.

One of the biggest challenges that my case interview coaching clients face, and that I faced with slide-making is one that I touched on earlier: balancing the constraints of limited time, speaking to and engaging your interviewer, and writing on your paper to create the slides. Managing this challenge is one of the key topics in the next chapter on communication and real-time problem-solving with your interviewer.

CHAPTER 7

Communication: Real-time Problem-Solving in Conversation

"They (the Good-to-Great companies) didn't use discussion as a sham process to let people 'have their say' so that they could 'buy in' to a predetermined decision. The process was more like a heated scientific debate, with people engaged in a search for the best answers."– Jim Collins, Good to Great: Why Some Companies Make the Leap... and Others Don't, *2001* [23]

This chapter's quote comes from the seminal book by Jim Collins (a former McKinsey consultant) based on a paired analysis of 11 companies that transitioned from having mediocre stock returns to providing stock returns that were several multiples better than the stock market average and doing so for a sustained period. It reflects the role that discussion has at consulting firms as well: a heated scientific debate with people engaged in a search for the best answers. One of McKinsey's core values is "to uphold the obligation to dissent" [8], meaning that there is an expectation that you should disagree with your colleagues in a debate.

View the interview conversation as a problem-solving session with your interviewer. You are the thought-leader since it is your project that you have ownership over. But don't discount the importance of communicating your thought process inclusively so that your interviewer can contribute to the discussion. Consultants are not know-it-all's; they work with their teammates and their clients to co-develop the best solution.

In this chapter, we'll walk through best practices for communicating with your interviewer during the case interview.

Section 7-1 Communication: what interviewers are looking for

There are 3 criteria that McKinsey uses to review its consultants that have implications for how you communicate during the case interview:

#	Criteria for evaluating consultants	Implications for case interview
1	Does this consultant ask the client for feedback and adjust their approach accordingly?	Be coachable. If the interviewer gives you a suggestion, modify your approach based on that feedback.
2	Does he write clear, concise emails?	Be clear and concise by using structure. Incorporate structure into your communication as much as possible.
3	Does he lead with key messages?	Share your conclusion or recommendation first. Then provide the supporting evidence.

Table 7-1 Criteria used by McKinsey to evaluate consultants' communication skills and what they mean for your approach to communication in the case interview.

The first point is self-explanatory. Be open-minded and don't show rigid thinking if the interviewer provides you with a suggestion.

I want to emphasize the second point. From an interviewer's perspective, it fatigues them to interview candidates back-to-back over the course of the day. It requires less energy for them to follow what you are saying if you can incorporate structure into your communication. That means that if you are at a stage where you're unable to respond to a question or provide next steps in a structured way, it is a worthwhile tradeoff to ask for time (no more than 30 seconds) to think first before responding. That way, the interviewer can take a mental break themselves and check their phone while you take a little time. They can then understand your subsequent structured communication more easily.

The third point is most consequential for the final recommendation, which we'll discuss in greater depth later in this chapter in Section 7-6.

Section 7-2 Communication as a thought-leader

Remember to stay in the mindset of being a hypothesis-driven problem-solver and thought leader–the type of confidence that a consultant brings to their clients. That means you may not have knowledge about the subject at hand, but you can structure problems, develop hypotheses, determine an approach to test those hypotheses, and drive to the next steps to carry out those steps. Since you may not have knowledge about the subject at hand, make sure you ask the basic background (or what we referred to as "stupid" in Section 4-2) questions.

Being able to structure problems, develop hypotheses, and determine an approach to test those hypotheses means that you should not ask your interviewer open-ended questions. For example, you should never ask, "Is there any other data that you have?" or "What data do you have?" because in consulting engagements, there is infinite data available in the form of people you can interview, the internet, public and paid databases, and so on. Instead, ask for the data you need to test a hypothesis, e.g., "This investment in this machine could reduce the need for certain raw materials. Do we have data on the types and costs of raw materials the client would need before and after we employ the machine?"

Section 7-3 Communication during Analytical questions

After the interviewer presents you the case prompt and you've finished going through your clarifying questions, it's time to create your structure and communicate that to the interviewer. You're facing the challenges of balancing the constraints of limited time, needing to draw up a structure, and then presenting it with sufficient depth while not taking too much time to do so. Here I'll walk you step-by-step through the structuring part of the interview with a focus on managing time and communication.

1. Ask for time. Never go into a pause without giving the interviewer a heads up and receiving their permission.
2. Take 1-2 minutes to yourself to draw your structure. You shouldn't need to think for too long here. Try to come up with the structure you want to use while you and the interviewer are talking through the clarifying questions. Draw up your structure, including the 2nd and maybe 3rd level sub-buckets. Jot down abbreviations to remind you of your hypothesis under each sub-bucket. Do not exceed 2 minutes of silence here.
3. Present your slide. Point to the buckets on your slide as you walk your interviewer through your structure. This way, if you are taking too long to walk through your structure, your interviewer can go off of your visual aid to re-direct you to talk about other buckets they're interested in. Being inclusive in this way enables a productive problem-solving session.
4. Talk through the structure. Present the high-level buckets and sub-buckets. Share which buckets you think will be most important ("Prioritize Analysis"). Then present one hypothesis for each sub-bucket to accomplish the "Plan Analyses" step of the 7-Step Problem-Solving Process.

Refer to the example dialogue in italics in Section 3-6 as an approach to mimic in your communication of your structure.

Section 7-4 Communication during Conceptual questions

Brainstorming

When the interviewer asks you a brainstorming question (which happens in both interviewer- and interviewee-led formats), you'll first run through your clarifying questions ("Define Problem"). Then I recommend the following steps for how you communicate:

1. Unless a structure comes to your mind immediately, ask for 30 seconds to yourself.
2. If you asked for time, take only 30 seconds. Draw up your structure. Do not write any brainstormed ideas under your buckets unless you think you'll forget them later.
3. Present your slide. By now your slide should just be a structure with no brainstormed ideas under the buckets. Point to the buckets on your slide and outline them for your interviewer. Share your hypothesis of what bucket you think will drive the most value for the client (Prioritize issues).
4. Walk through the brainstorming with the interviewer. Begin with the first bucket, then list as many ideas in that bucket as possible off the top of your head to the interviewer. You need not write them down, just verbalize them. Repeat for the other buckets. (Plan Analyses—partially)
5. After completing brainstorming, you want to do another iteration of the "Prioritize Analysis" step if you believe that a few of your brainstormed ideas are impractical or low value, and you want to make that clear to your interviewer.

Refer to the example dialogue in italics in Section 4-3 as an approach to mimic when the interviewer asks you a brainstorming question.

Exhibit interpretation

When the interviewer slides an exhibit across the table and asks you to tell them what you make of it, or asks you a specific question, your communication approach differs a little from brainstorming questions because the structuring step is more straightforward for exhibits, so you should be able to structure on the fly. As we discussed in Section 2-6 and Section 4-4, the structure that you use to extract insights for exhibit interpretation questions is most often going to be the rows or columns of the exhibit, the overarching structure used for the case, or a structure based on the specific question that the interviewer asked you pertaining to the exhibit.

Let's walk through the steps of your communication for exhibit interpretation:

1. Define Problem: ask any clarifying questions needed in order to get specific about the goal of this exhibit interpretation question. What financial metrics are we focused on? Are there any words or metrics that the interviewer used that you need to ask them to define?
2. Structure: explain to the interviewer that you will structure your approach to extracting insights from the exhibit and explain what you based your structure on. Is it the overarching structure for the case, the rows or columns of the exhibit itself, or did you create a new structure?
3. Prioritize issues: share your hypothesis of which buckets of your structure are more significant.
4. Plan analysis: Ask for 30 seconds if you think it'll help you extract more out of the exhibit. Jot down some notes if you think that will help you recall certain things when you speak again. But don't take over 30 seconds of silence here.
5. Conduct analysis: Walk the interviewer through your observations from the exhibit, going one bucket at a time through your structure. There's no need to write anything down at this point.

You just need to verbalize as many observations as you can in each one of your buckets to the interviewer.

6. Synthesize analysis: wrap up your exhibit interpretation by giving your interviewer your thoughts about what this exhibit means overall to the client.
7. Develop recommendation: share the next steps you want to take. What updated hypotheses do you have, and how do you want to test them to provide the client with a recommendation?

Refer to the example dialogue in italics in Section 4-4 as an approach to mimic when the interviewer asks you to interpret an exhibit.

Section 7-5 Communication during Quantitative questions

Talking through math calculations in real-time is challenging for many of my coaching clients. However, do not carry out all of your calculations in silence because it is helpful to have the interviewer following your calculations so they can catch any errors you make early on. Otherwise, if you make an error while doing your calculations in silence, the interviewer needs to troubleshoot your calculation with you after you present your final answer to them.

Furthermore, it is important to keep the interviewer engaged during your interview and not let too much time pass in silence. Otherwise, the interviewer might perceive you as not being able to think on your feet. Consultants need to develop Excel spreadsheets in real-time during problem-solving sessions while being watched by senior partners via WebEx or in-person. If you can't do that with calculations using pen and paper during the case interview, that would be problematic if they were to hire you.

The best way to develop this skill of being able to talk through your math while calculating is practice, which we'll discuss in more detail in Chapter 8 and Chapter 9.

The other important point about communication during math questions that I want to emphasize up front is confidence in your calculations.

Never ask "is that right?" at the end of one of your calculations because a consultant would never ask their client if their work is right.

It's acceptable to ask for 30 seconds to work in silence to develop a structure to show to the interviewer. However, as mentioned earlier, talk through the actual calculations.

Here I want to walk you through how I'd talk to the interviewer through the math for an example case [24]:

Interviewer: Your client is a real estate private equity firm. They have asked you to calculate the net present value (NPV) for purchasing a property and developing a series of golf villas on it. The property is 250 acres in Colorado. Each golf villa will be half an acre in size, and the golf villas overall will take up half of the property. It will cost $100,000 to develop each villa, $2.5M for the roads and infrastructure, $2.5M for the clubhouse, and $5M for the golf course. Weekly rentals will cost $2,000 in the winter and summer; and $1,000 in the fall and spring. Occupancy rates will be 100% in the summer and winter, and 67% in the fall and spring. Assume that each season is 12 weeks long. Maintenance costs are $1M annually and start in year 2.

(Step 1: Define Problem)

Me: I see. The objective of the calculation is to determine the NPV for this project. It sounds like you listed all the upfront investment costs except the cost to acquire the property itself. Do we want to include those costs in the analysis? In addition, it sounds like this cash flow from the property will continue in perpetuity. Is that right or do we expect to sell the property at some point?

Interviewer: Great point, let's include the cost to acquire the property. Let's say it is $15M. Assume that we keep the property and expect the cash flow in perpetuity. It may be helpful for you to know that the present value of a constant cash flow in perpetuity is the annual cash flow divided by the discount rate as a decimal.

(Step 2: Structure Problem)

Me: Got it. Can I take about 30 seconds to draw up a structure for how to approach this calculation?

Interviewer: Go for it.

Me: Thank you.

(30-second period of silence)

Me: I've sketched up this structure here (shows slide). To calculate the NPV, there are three major components: Investment costs, Cash flow, and Discount rate.

The investment costs are all 1-time costs upfront. There are 2 main investment cost categories. The cost to acquire, which is $15M. My understanding is that this cost includes any closing costs, transaction fees, or inspection costs. Then there are development costs, which break into golf course, golf villas, clubhouse, and roads and other infrastructure.

The next top-level bucket (points to next bucket on slide) is the Cash Flow. These are all recurring annual cash flow items. The Cash Flow breaks into Revenue and Cost. On the Revenue side, the only revenues are from the winter/summer and fall/spring season categories, which both have their differing occupancy rates and weekly prices. My understanding is that these prices include any other revenue streams on the property such as parking, food, gift shop and so on. In Costs, there are no variable costs, and the fixed costs are all accounted for in the $1M annual maintenance cost you mentioned.

There is also the discount rate, which we'd use in the denominator of the perpetuity equation.

(Step 3: Prioritize issues)

The most significant area for analysis will be the revenue. It's not clear that with mediocre occupancy rates for half the year we'll be able to break-even to have a positive NPV.

Interviewer: Okay. I agree with the assumptions you made. Let's say that the discount rate is 25%.

(Step 4: Plan analyses)

Me: Got it, okay. I'm going to first calculate the total 1-time investment costs. Then I will calculate the cash flow and resulting perpetuity from the discount rate. I'll net out the 1-time investment costs from the perpetuity to get the NPV.

(Step 5: Conduct analyses)

First, the 1-time investment costs. I will create a table here on my new slide. I'm writing the objective at the top of the page: NPV in dollars. For the 1-time investment costs, the rows of my table will be Acquisition costs, Golf course, villas, Clubhouse, Roads, and infrastructure. The Acquisition cost is $15M. The golf course is $5M, the roads are $2.5M and the clubhouse is $2.5M. The villas cost depends on the number of villas which I haven't determined yet.

So I'll make another table below this one to determine that. The total acreage of the property is 250. We will use half of that for the villas so 125. Each villa is half an acre. So the total villas that will fit is 125 acres over 0.5 acres. I'm doing this calculation here on my scratch paper. 125 acres divided by 0.5 acres per villa. The acres unit cancels in the numerator and denominator, and the "villa" unit comes into the numerator. The division gives me 2 times 125 which equals 250. So 250 total villas, which I'll transfer back into my table on my slide.

Each villa costs $100,000 to develop. So the total villa development cost is 250 times $100k. That gives me "25,000k" or $25M. That makes sense comparing to the cost of the golf course. Another way to think of it is that each villa costs $0.1M to develop for 250 villas which gives $25M.

I'll transfer that $25M back into my 1-time costs table. I'll total up the various 1-time costs now. $25M plus $5M plus $2.5M plus $2.5M plus $15M. That is 25 plus 10 plus 15. Or 35 plus 15. So that total 1-time cost is $50M.

Moving on to the cash flow now. The revenue, as I mentioned before, is my biggest concern because of the mediocre occupancy rates during half the year. What I'll do is calculate the average weekly revenue per room for both of the 2 season-categories. Then I'll average the two and scale up by the number of villas to get average weekly revenue for the entire property. Then scale up by 48 weeks to get total annual revenue. This way I minimize the number of multiplication operations I need to do.

So I'm setting up my table to have one column for summer-winter and one column for spring-fall. The rows will be average weekly revenue per room, occupancy rate, and price per room.

First let's consider winter-summer, the strong seasons. The price is $2000, and the occupancy is 100%. So the average weekly revenue per room is the product of the two, or $2000. Moving on to the next column: spring-fall, the weaker seasons. The price is $1000 and the occupancy rate is 67%. So the average weekly revenue per room is $1000 times 67% or $670.

In my next table, I'll have average weekly revenue per room over the year. Then number of rooms. Then number of weeks per year. The average weekly revenue per room over the year is the average of the 2 season-categories, or the average of $670 and $2000. I'll calculate that here on my scratch paper. The sum of the two is $2670. Dividing that by 2 gives me $1335. Next I'll multiply that by the number of rooms on the property which we found earlier was 250. So 250 times $1335. That's equivalent to one-fourth of $1335 times 1000. One-fourth of $1335 is 333.75. Let me just check that real quick: 4 times 333.75 is 1335, so that makes sense. Multiplying 333.75 times 1000 gives $333,750. So the average revenue per week across the year for the entire property is $333,750. That makes sense.

Let me scale this up by the 48 weeks in the year. 48 times $333,750. I will round the 48 up to 50 since that makes the math simpler and is closer to the number of weeks in a year. So 50 times $333,750, which is equivalent to 100 times $333,750 over 2. 100 times $333,750 is $33.375M. Dividing that by 2 gives $16.687M. Since we are roughly estimating the occupancy rates anyway, I will round this number to $16.7M.

So the total revenue per year will be $16.7M. Subtracting out the maintenance cost gives $15.7M as the annual cash flow. Dividing that by 25%

to get the perpetuity is equivalent to multiplying by 4. So 15.7 times 4 is \$62.8M perpetuity cash flow.

Let's compare that to the upfront costs, which we calculated earlier to be \$50M. When I net that out of the cash perpetuity, we find that the total NPV is \$12.8M.

(Step 6: Synthesize analyses)

As a percentage of the upfront investment, that is about one-quarter or 25%. I think that is a good return.

(Step 7: Develop recommendation)

I'd recommend that the client move forward with this project. As next steps, we could look into how to drive greater revenue during the down seasons of spring and fall.

Interviewer: Thanks.

I wanted to walk you through that conversation to see how I'd talk the interviewer through the math calculations in Step 5 (Conduct Analysis). I would show the interviewer my slide the entire time. This way I keep them engaged and they can also catch any minor errors I make, and so that it is not energy intensive for them to do so. We all make math mistakes (I made one in my final round with McKinsey), but if your manager can feel that you are communicating with clarity so that the two of you together can catch mistakes before they grow into headaches, then she will feel comfortable adding you to her team.

Section 7-6 Final recommendations

There are two main considerations I want you to take into account whenever you provide your interviewer with your final recommendation when she simulates the ride with the CEO in the elevator: (1) leading with key message and (2) Situation-Complication-Resolution (SCR) framework for communication.

First, as mentioned in Section 7-1, one criterion that McKinsey assesses consultants based on is whether they lead with key messages. This means that when they communicate an idea to a more senior person or to a client, that they begin the communication with the key point first, before sharing supporting details or minutiae.

What this means for you in the case interview is that when asked for your final recommendation to the CEO, first start off sharing the most important points from her perspective as CEO. Do you have a recommendation for what they should do? If you are not sure about your recommendation because you have some other analysis that you need to do, say that. Tell them you are leaning towards Option A as the best option for them because of a few data points you've uncovered, but you still have to assess a few more things before finalizing the recommendation.

Second, make sure you use the SCR (Situation-Complication-Resolution) framework [25], which is a communication structure that McKinsey advocates among its consultants:

- **S**ituation: reminding the audience of the context that they already know to level-set them on the same page before you introduce fresh information.
- **C**omplication: the problem.
- **R**esolution: the solution to the problem (including the recommendation and next steps of analysis).

Applying the SCR framework means that you should remind the CEO of the project you are working on before you give the recommendation.

Let's now bring both points together and run through an example. I want to return to the jet manufacturer case that we introduced in Section 5-3 and worked through the math for in Figure 5-1.

Interviewer: Let's say that the CEO comes into the team-room to say hi. While there, she asks how things are going. What would you say?

Me: Okay. Hello CEO, as you know, the company is trying to determine the location for its next manufacturing plant: the US, Argentina or Italy. We were brought in to determine which option will generate the highest profit for the company. It's looking like the best option is to build the plant in the US. The 5-year profit for the US is $16B, just a shade under the $16.5B in profit we'd get in Argentina. So the US almost provides as much profit but it has much less geopolitical risk than Argentina. Italy provides substantially less profit than the US so we have ruled it out. To complete our recommendation, we will dive into vetting the risks factors involved in the US versus Argentina.

Interviewer: Great, thanks. We're done with the case. What questions do you have for me?

There you see that I gave the CEO a brief reminder of who I am and what problem I am working on for her company. I then next gave my most important conclusion—that they should build the plant in the US—followed by my reasoning and next steps.

Section 7-7 Communication in the Interviewer- vs Interviewee-led formats

The interviewer vs interviewee-led formats feel different. But if you are preparing for the interviewer-led format, I urge you to not fall into the trap of neglecting Steps 6 and 7 of the Problem-Solving Process: synthesize to determine the "so what" for the client, based on the analysis you did in response to the question asked, and then develop a recommendation or next steps based on that synthesis. I can't stress this enough because one criterion that McKinsey uses to review its consultants is that they do not wait to be told what to do. That means that in the interviewer-led format, you don't wait to be asked the next question, but you attempt to predict what that next question needs to be for our team to deliver client impact.

If you are preparing for the interviewee-led format, then leverage Steps 6 and 7 to drive to the next phase of analysis. After you present your upfront structure and prioritize analyses, plan and conduct analyses based on that prioritization. Then once you conduct an analysis such as interpreting an exhibit or calculating a quantity, synthesize the "so what" and lay out the next steps to get to a recommendation.

You should base the next steps to get to the recommendation on your upfront structure. What are the other areas in your structure that you planned upfront as requiring analysis but that you have learned nothing about yet? Lay all of those things out as the next steps. Then prioritize them and move on to the highest priority area to plan and conduct analyses. The 7-Step Problem-Solving Process is iterative, so rinse and repeat.

Section 7-8 What should you do if you get stuck?

When I first began preparing for case interviews, my biggest fear was what would happen if I got stuck. When this happens, think about what you'd do if you were leading a team that had gotten stuck. Go to the whiteboard and lay out what you know and what you need to find out. Refer back to your structure and your notes so far about what you've learned.

What you're doing is running through the 7 steps of the problem-solving process again. Remind yourself, what's the goal we are after (Define Problem)? What do we need to find out (Structure Problem)? What do we think is the next big issue we need to learn about (Prioritize Issues)? That should guide you to what analyses you need to do next.

When you get stuck, it's okay to ask for 30 seconds to collect your thoughts to go through these steps. But don't show any other signs that you are stuck such as admitting that you are stuck.

We've introduced the concepts for problem-solving and habits of communications. Theory alone, however, will not make you successful at the case interview. Case interview performance requires practice just like developing your performance in any sport. The last part of this book will be a guide to how to train to succeed on interview day.

Your prep for interviewer- vs interviewee-led formats should differ in 3 key ways

Interviewee-led challenge
Interviewer-led challenge

Challenge	Mitigation approach	Implementation and rationale
Anxiety of awkward silences on interviewee-led (similar to awkward silences on a 1st date)	(1) Ingrain habits of: a) Prioritizing issues/analyses and b) Developing recommendations throughout interviewee-led interviews.	a) You'll naturally lay out the most important task in front of us, and therefore will confidently state next step. b) You'll naturally either recommend a course of action or identify what gaps that need to be filled to get there.
	(2) Acclimate to rhythm of interviewee-led format	Repeated simulated mock case interviews with practice partner. Let partner know that you'd like to practice interviewee-led format.
Perceived expectations for distinct steps of problem-solving process	(3) Ingrain the same 2 habits from point #1. When concluding response to any type question, be sure to: a) Prioritizing issues/analyses and b) Developing recommendations	In interviewer-led, candidate tends to answer question being asked w/o interpreting answer's implications for the client, e.g., calculating a numerical response w/o interpreting the number. In the interviewer-led format, make sure you follow-up your response to any question (e.g., numerical computation) with (a) the most important next step, and (b) recommendation or the gap that exists to identifying a recommendation.

ONSIGHT CASE INTERVIEW COACHING

Onsightcasecoaching.com
manu@onsightcasecoaching.com

Figure 7-1 Summary of how your preparation should differ slightly for interviewer- vs interviewee-led case interview formats.

PART III

Training and Game Plan

CHAPTER 8

Working out and training: solo drills to refine your skills

"The fight is won or lost far away from witnesses - behind the lines, in the gym, and out there on the road, long before I dance under those lights."–Muhammad Ali [26]

The key phrase I want to highlight in this chapter's opening quote is "away from witnesses." And the corresponding key word that I want highlight in the chapter title is "solo."

A mistake I made when I went through the consulting interview process the first time—my unsuccessful attempt—was that my only practice was simulated mock case interviews with friends. I did not do enough isolated practice by myself.

When a basketball player practices her jump shot in the driveway by herself, she can focus more on the specifics of her form: keeping her elbow perpendicular to the rim, the timing of the release, the locking of her eyes on the rim, calibration of the feel of the flick of her wrist, and so on. In the same way, you need to practice the problem-solving skills and habits that I've laid out for you in Part I and Part II by yourself with a focus on the specifics. In this chapter, I'll lay out the drills that you can do by yourself to win the fight "far away from witnesses."

Section 8-1 How to plan your training regimen

The best way to plan your training regimen is to do so iteratively based on feedback. In Chapter 9, we'll discuss how to get that feedback in simulated mock case interviews. Here I want to emphasize that you should pay close attention to that feedback and revise your training regimen based on it.

To start out, I'd recommend selecting the exercises from this chapter that take you 15 minutes or fewer and do all of those for at least one repetition per day. For exercises that take longer than 15 minutes, start off doing one repetition every other day. Then as you receive feedback from your mock interview partners, use that feedback to adjust the frequency of your exercise repetitions.

Being self-aware is critical here. Can you listen to the feedback you are receiving and take it to heart?

I also want to emphasize that when setting your training regimen, do not assume any immediate strengths or weaknesses when you are starting out. For example, I did my undergraduate degree in physics and my PhD in Biomedical Engineering. Although my educational training provided me with natural strengths, I still needed to practice my quantitative problem-solving. I needed isolated dedicated practice to get the hang of making slides and tables for math questions; and getting comfortable doing math calculations by hand and talking through the math with an interviewer watching me. Because of my natural strengths, however, I could get up to speed on the math relatively quickly, at which point I shifted my focus to areas where I did not have natural strengths such as creativity.

For a suggested practice schedule, refer to the one laid out in Section 1-4. However, I believe the most important aspect of your preparation is not the time spent, but how *self-aware* and *deliberate* you are in your practice.

Section 8-2 Considerations for non-MBA's

As we discussed in Section 1-5, there are two potential disadvantages that non-MBA's come into case interview preparation with: (1) Less likelihood of having memorized basic business concepts, and (2) Less likelihood of genuinely enjoying discussing business concepts. If you are a non-MBA, there are things that you should do to mitigate these two risks.

Regarding the first point, spend more time memorizing the generic frameworks that I laid out in Section 3-2 using flash cards (print off our flash cards at onsightcasecoaching.com/blogs/news/flash-cards/), as I will discuss in the next section (Section 8-3). Also, you must pay special attention in the clarifying questions part of the interview to make sure you ask "stupid" questions as discussed in Section 4-2 to ensure you understand the client's business sufficiently before you dive into problem-solving mode.

Regarding the second point about enjoying discussing business, if you are someone with a technical engineering type of background who may not have as much of a deep appreciation for creative work, I recommend that you spend more time repeating the exercises that involve using business periodicals that I will lay out in the next two sections (Section 8-3 and Section 8-4). These exercises will help you appreciate how creative thinking can have a real impact on business problems that companies in the news are facing today.

Now if you're someone with a more humanities-type of background who may not have as much of a deep appreciation for quantitative analysis, I recommend that you spend more time repeating the math exercise described in Section 8-5. When you are able to repeat this exercise with accurate math, you'll develop an appreciation for the insights that you can drive from organized math tables with quantitative analysis.

Non-business degree holders can mitigate their 2 disadvantages in a short period of time with practice

Disadvantage	SAT/ACT metaphor	Case interview analogue	How to mitigate
(1) **Memorization of basic business concepts**	HS seniors who've taken precalculus are more likely to have memorized geometry principles tested on the SAT such as complementary angles	Business majors are more likely to have memorized basic business concepts such as what to consider in market entry, M&A, etc.	Memorize generic frameworks of checklists to consider in common business scenarios such as market entry, M&A, etc.
(2) **Appreciation for working on business problems**	HS seniors who've taken precalculus are more likely to genuinely enjoy math topics tested on the SAT such as geometry and algebra	Technical majors: may lack confidence or appreciation for creativity and qualitative structuring problems in business. Humanities majors: may lack confidence or appreciation for quantitative analysis in business.	Technical majors: use the *Wall Street Journal* or other business periodical to practice brainstorming and qualitative structuring regularly. Humanities majors: work on math problem from a case in a casebook from start to finish with special emphasis on structuring methodology and making clean numerical tables.

Figure 8-1 Summary of how non-MBA's should prepare differently for the case interview versus their MBA peers.

Section 8-3 Analytical problem-solving exercises

Flash cards for generic frameworks

To memorize the 6 generic frameworks in Section 3-2, you can make flashcards (or print off ours at onsightcasecoaching.com/blogs/news/flash-cards/) to test your memory recall. On one side of each flash card, write the name of the framework (e.g., "Entering a New Market"), and on the other side draw the framework. When you review the flashcards, stack them in such a way that the side of the cards facing up is the name of the structure. When you review a particular flashcard, after you see the name of the structure, pull out a sheet of paper and sketch the structure out from memory. Then flip the card over to compare your drawing to the correct answer. This way you practice being able to draw the structure out from memory in the same fashion you would in the interview.

Cycle through your flash cards. Put away the cards you answer correctly on your first try. Then continue to review the cards that could not recall until you get those correct as well.

You may find it more effective to adjust these frameworks in your own way as you practice cases, then memorize your tailored frameworks. It's much easier to memorize or remember a framework that you've tailored based on your own experiences than just remembering a framework thrust upon you by a book like this one.

You may also want to include a flash card in your review for how to apply the 7-Step Problem-Solving Process during upfront structuring and for the SCR (situation-complication-resolution) structure for final recommendations.

Structuring exercise

My favorite exercises are the ones that involve applying your problem-solving skills to business problems that companies are facing right now. This is one of those exercises.

Open up a business periodical such as the *Financial Times*, the *Wall Street Journal* or the *Economist*. Skip the politics section, go to the business section and browse the headlines to find one about a scenario that a consulting firm may help a client with. Don't read the article yet, but make sure you understand the general problem being described. In your mind, define who the client is and complete the "Define Problem" step as if you were pretending they were your client. Once you've done that, turn your timer on for 2 minutes and draw up a structure. Present that structure to an imaginary interviewer.

Next, grade yourself on how you did. A few questions that you can ask to grade your performance are:

- Read the article. Did it touch on any considerations you did not touch on in your structure?
- Did your presentation include one hypothesis under each sub-bucket? Would it be an engaging presentation in that it included hypotheses that would interest a CEO-level audience? Or was it a laundry list of questions that are more appropriate to communicate to a research analyst to whom you are delegating work?
- Did you prioritize by sharing a hypothesis of which bucket is the most important for analysis?
- Was your structure MECE? (See Section 3-1 if you forgot what "MECE" means).

This exercise develops your ability to generate hypotheses for a specific client scenario. If you cannot approach the problem using a generic framework, then this exercise also builds your skill in creating customized frameworks.

I enjoy using current business problems because they allow you to develop a deeper appreciation for the problem-solving skills tested on the case interview as you see how they can apply right now to generate value for potential clients. They also help you deepen your business intuition as you think more about varying issues and considerations companies face today. For example, you may come across price discrimination used by a pharmaceutical company and think through the pros and cons of doing that. You may come across a story about a startup company whose founders left after it got acquired, and the risks involved for the acquiring company when that happens.

Every day, you can find several articles to practice with. For example:

- an article about Disney having doubled its subscribers for its streaming service could form the basis of a hypothetical case question about how you could help Netflix respond;
- an article about Stryker considering taking over Boston Scientific could be turned into a case about Stryker asking for your advice whether it should proceed with that acquisition;
- an article about the mining industry broadly facing challenges due to the electrification of vehicles could be turned into a case about a mining client needing your help to define its strategy in response to that industry trend.

In addition, my case interview coaching clients have found RocketBlocks (http://rocketblocks.me) to be a helpful tool to practice structuring and brainstorming exercises.

Final recommendation exercise

Being able to give articulate final recommendations was challenging for me when I began practicing cases. An exercise that worked well for me to improve was to look at past cases—that I'd practiced in a simulated mock interview with a friend or that I'd practiced the math for—and then ask myself, "if I could type up my final recommendation for the CEO, how would that look?" I'd then take some time to plan what a good recommendation would look like.

This exercise is easier than what you have to do in an actual case interview where you have to come up with a recommendation on the spot or with 30 seconds of silence. But it's like a basketball player who practices wide open jump shots in the gym to prepare to make those shots with a defender guarding them under pressure. If you can master the easier scenario, it can help you with the more challenging one.

When you grade your typed-out recommendation, ask yourself the following questions:

- Did the recommendation start with some brief context for the CEO?
- Did the recommendation provide the main conclusion or recommendation before providing supporting evidence or methodology?
- Did the recommendation end with some next steps to manage risk or to strengthen the recommendation?

Section 8-4 Conceptual problem-solving exercises

Brainstorming exercise

The brainstorming exercise is another where you can use articles from a business periodical to work on a business problem a company is facing. Repeat the steps from the structuring exercise above where you open up a business periodical and find an article. The difference here is that instead of pretending that you are structuring the problem, you now pretend that you are brainstorming solutions to a specific question. If I take the three example articles I laid out earlier in the structuring exercise section, example questions for brainstorming could be:

- What specific initiatives can your client, Netflix, do to take market share from Disney's streaming service?
- What specific potential risks exist that Stryker should keep in mind when acquiring Boston Scientific?
- What specific ways will vehicle electrification impact our mining client?

Once you've defined the brainstorming question, turn on your timer for 30 seconds, and draw up a structure. Prioritize which bucket is most important, then walk your imaginary interviewer through your brainstorming of your responses to the question using each bucket in your structure.

Then grade yourself by asking yourself these questions:

- Did you come up with at least 7 mutually exclusive brainstormed ideas?
- Was your structure helpful for your brainstorming and was it exhaustive?
- Read the article. Were there any ideas in the article that you didn't come up with in your brainstorming?

As with structuring, you may find RocketBlocks to be a useful tool for practicing brainstorming.

Exhibit interpretation exercise

For exhibit interpretation, it's best to use exhibits designed for case interviews in casebooks. You can find casebooks by using the links in the Bibliography section of this book. Most of these casebooks that I have cited are freely available at the URLs listed in the Bibliography. In addition, you must find casebooks for the math exercise in Section 8-5 and for simulated mock interviews with your practice partners as described in Chapter 9. If you need the Bibliography in electronic format, email me (manu@OnsightCaseCoaching.com) or visit onsightcasecoaching.com/blogs/news/casebooks.

In any casebook, flip to any random case in the book you haven't read or worked on yet. Read through the background prompt and then find the first exhibit in the case. Practice going through all 7 steps of the Problem-Solving Process for interpreting the exhibit as I described in Section 4-4. Then grade yourself by asking yourself the following questions:

- Were there any insights in the solution key that you missed in your interpretation of the exhibit?

- Did you synthesize your insights to articulate the overall "so what" for the client?
- Did you conclude by developing a recommendation for the client or next steps to test your hypothesis of the recommendation?

Flash cards

Add to your flash card deck the following four flash cards:

1. SMART: How to use the SMART acronym to define the objective for a project from Section 2-3
2. VOM acronym from Section 4-2
3. How to apply the 7-Step Problem-Solving Process for brainstorming questions from Section 4-3
4. How to apply the 7-Step Problem-Solving Process for exhibit interpretation questions from Section 4-4

You can also print these flash cards off at onsightcasecoaching.com/blogs/news/flash-cards/. Test your memory recall using these flash cards whenever you review your others on generic frameworks.

Section 8-5 Quantitative problem-solving exercises

The only quantitative problem-solving exercise that I recommend is going through full math questions from casebooks. While going through math questions, focus on creating good slides and clean, accurate calculations without error. As I mentioned in Section 5-6, mental math is overrated and therefore you need not do any mental math drills.

As for the exhibit interpretation exercise, you must find casebooks for this math exercise. Find a case in the casebook (onsightcasecoaching.com/blogs/news/casebooks) you haven't read or done yet. Then read the case prompt to make sure you understand the background. Find the math question in the case and read only the question before you move on to applying the 7 steps of the Problem-Solving Process as described in Chapter 5 to answer the question. You may need to refer back to the case book as you recognize that there are pieces of data you need. But be careful not to read any parts of the solution. Make sure you lay out what data you need in your framework before you refer back to the casebook to get those pieces of data.

Once you complete the 7 steps, grade yourself using the following rubric:

- Did you write the objective—both the goal of the calculation and the units that the number should be in—at the top of your slide?
- Did you structure your approach before you started working with actual numbers?
- Did you use clean tables for calculating so that an interviewer could follow it?
- Did you contain all of your computations (e.g., multiplication signs, long multiplication, long division) to a separate scratch sheet of paper so it doesn't clutter your slide?
- Did you synthesize your final answer to articulate a "so what" for the client?
- Did you develop a final recommendation for the client or the next steps to test your hypothesis recommendation?

Flash cards

Add to your existing flash card deck (or print from onsightcasecoaching.com/blogs/news/flashcards/) one card on the three math structures that we reviewed in Section 5-3: "Current-state vs Future-state," "Market-sizing," and "Timeline."

I've given you quite a few solo drills and exercises in this chapter. You need not do every one of them every day, but make sure you have some rotation where you refine your weak areas. Your biggest gains will come from solo practice where you focus on your own development.

Let's now move on to the simulated mock cases, which will allow you to develop your habits of communication and to get feedback on your weak points.

CHAPTER 9

Scrimmages: partner cases

"Nothing brings two people closer together than weeks of debate prep. John, I'm looking forward to working with you instead of debating you." – Barack Obama at press conference announcing appointment of John Kerry as Secretary of State, December 21st, 2012 [27]

One type of test that somewhat parallels the case interview is preparation for a presidential debate. It's well known that candidates running for President of the United States will practice using mock debates with another politician role-playing as the opposing candidate through the summer as they prepare for the debate held close to the election in November. In the same way, I recommend you simulate mock interviews with a partner role-playing as the interviewer.

Barack Obama—regardless of whether you agree with his views and politics—made an effective decision in having John Kerry role-play as the Republican nominee Mitt Romney for debate practice. Kerry was someone who had deep expertise with the presidential debate stage because he ran for president himself in 2004 as the Democratic nominee. Likewise, I urge you to find someone to role-play as your interviewer who has knowledge of the case interview. I'll describe more on how to find that person in Section 9-1.

Another reason it was a good selection by Obama to have Kerry role-play as Romney is because as he mentions in the quote, the two of them became close friends while practicing, which served their working relationship well when Kerry became Obama's Secretary of State later that year when Obama was preparing his second-term cabinet. I became close friends with my case practice partners, and those friendships served us well in exchanging case interview tips, feedback, and advice after we became consultants. Let's discuss how you can find the right people to help you in preparing for the case interview and beyond.

Section 9-1 Finding good case practice partners

As I mentioned above, when you look for a case practice partner, you want to find someone who has knowledge about the case interview. The most likely category of people with that knowledge who will also be motivated to practice with you are other people who are preparing for the case interview like you are. To find these people, there are 5 broad categories of methods I'd recommend:

- University resources
  - o University Consulting clubs. This is how I found case practice partners early on. My university had a consulting club for advanced degree holders [28]. When I served on the executive board as the social chair, I got to know my fellow executive board members well and began practicing with them. At McKinsey, I had a close friend whose university did not have such a club. He did not let that discourage him, however. He found a university a few hours away that had a consulting club, and he would make the trip there for its weekly meetings so he could meet case practice partners. He met enough friends that he could practice cases with them online and he didn't have to make the lengthy drives anymore. It worked out well for him as he is an Engagement Manager at McKinsey today.

  - Career center. You might check with your career center to see if they have a way to connect you with others in your university who are also seeking a job in consulting.
- Consulting firms
  - Application-based recruiting events. This was by far my greatest source of case practice partners through the Bridge to BCG and McKinsey Insight programs [29] [30]. Consulting firms often host immersive programs for potential recruits where you can meet potential case practice partners.
  - Open recruiting events. Find out if any consulting firms are holding information sessions (virtual or in-person) that you can attend. Seek the other attendees using the chat feature of the video-conference platform or by approaching people during the networking part of the event. You can also do this at career fairs that are hosting consulting firms.
  - Recruiter. Ask the recruiters at consulting firms if they can connect you to other applicants to practice case interviews. It's in their best interest because the more you practice, the stronger their applicant pool.
- Free online resources. Several websites help you find case practice partners:
  - https://www.preplounge.com/en/case-interview-partner.php
  - https://www.caseinterviewpartner.com
  - https://www.consultingcase101.com/case-interview-practice-partners/case-partner-2019/
  - https://www.wallstreetoasis.com/forum/consulting
  - https://www.facebook.com/groups/355798371113012
  - https://consultingchallenge.org/case-partners-database/
- Coaching service
  - Pay a coaching service. We'll talk more about this option in Section 9-4.
  - If you have a coach already, ask your existing coach to connect you to her other clients.

- Existing partners
    - o Ask them to connect you to their other partners.

Once you find a partner, you can find cases to use when you are their mock interviewer through the casebooks I've linked to in the Bibliography section of this book. As I mentioned earlier, you can get the Bibliography in electronic format by emailing me (manu@OnsightCaseCoaching.com) or visiting onsightcasecoaching.com/blogs/news/casebooks/.

Section 9-2 Scoring rubric to ask your partner to use when interviewing you

Schedule recurring (we'll discuss the frequency in Section 9-5) meetings with your case practice partners—either virtual or in-person. Switch off between role-playing as the interviewer and interviewee.

When you are the interviewee, it's in your best interest to provide your case practice partner with some input on how you want them to provide you with feedback. You can ask them to fill out the 2-page form in Figure 9-1 and Figure 9-2.

You'll notice that in Figure 9-2, I advise the interviewer to attempt to "tie comments here to the interviewee's prior performances." To help your interviewer do that, make sure that before you begin the mock interview, you give them some context on your strengths and weaknesses. If they've practiced with you before, you can remind them of your performance the last time you practiced together.

Remember to always receive feedback with gratitude, as opposed to defending yourself. Otherwise, your case practice partners may hesitate to share honest feedback with you, which would be your loss. You can still take their feedback with a grain of salt, but always encourage your partners to share their observations with candor.

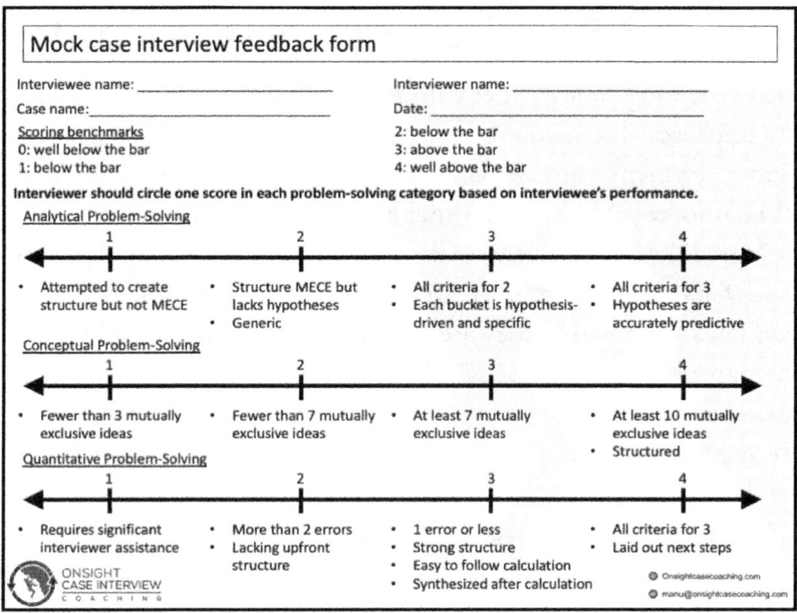

Mock case interview feedback form

Interviewee name: ____________________ Interviewer name: ____________________

Case name: ____________________ Date: ____________________

Scoring benchmarks
0: well below the bar
1: below the bar
2: below the bar
3: above the bar
4: well above the bar

Interviewer should circle one score in each problem-solving category based on interviewee's performance.

Analytical Problem-Solving

1	2	3	4
• Attempted to create structure but not MECE	• Structure MECE but lacks hypotheses • Generic	• All criteria for 2 • Each bucket is hypothesis-driven and specific	• All criteria for 3 • Hypotheses are accurately predictive

Conceptual Problem-Solving

1	2	3	4
• Fewer than 3 mutually exclusive ideas	• Fewer than 7 mutually exclusive ideas	• At least 7 mutually exclusive ideas	• At least 10 mutually exclusive ideas • Structured

Quantitative Problem-Solving

1	2	3	4
• Requires significant interviewer assistance	• More than 2 errors • Lacking upfront structure	• 1 error or less • Strong structure • Easy to follow calculation • Synthesized after calculation	• All criteria for 3 • Laid out next steps

ONSIGHT CASE INTERVIEW COACHING

Onsightcasecoaching.com
manu@onsightcasecoaching.com

Figure 9-1 Feedback form for partner mock case interviews, page 1.

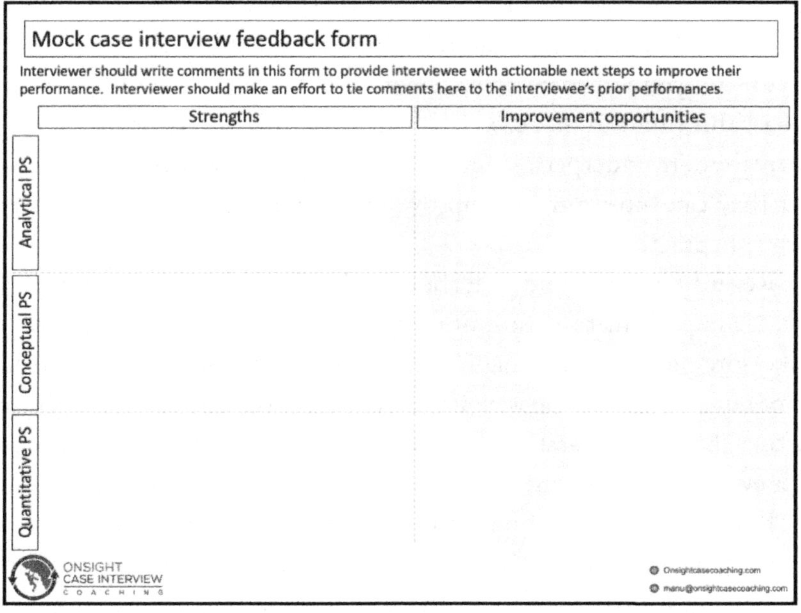

Mock case interview feedback form

Interviewer should write comments in this form to provide interviewee with actionable next steps to improve their performance. Interviewer should make an effort to tie comments here to the interviewee's prior performances.

	Strengths	Improvement opportunities
Analytical PS		
Conceptual PS		
Quantitative PS		

ONSIGHT CASE INTERVIEW COACHING

Onsightcasecoaching.com
manu@onsightcasecoaching.com

Figure 9-2 Feedback form for partner mock case interviews, page 2.

Section 9-3 Providing feedback to your partner

When providing your partner with feedback, your two goals are to help them improve—it's in your best interest to work with strong partners—and to make them enjoy working with you so they'll continue to do so as well as connect you with their other case practice partners.

Regarding the first goal, make sure you use the feedback forms in Figure 9-1 and Figure 9-2. Be honest about the score you give because if you tell someone that they are "above the bar," and they subsequently don't pass their case interviews, that reflects poorly on your judgement and standard. If you score them "below the bar," that is feedback for them to keep improving and as a result they will be more likely to pass their case interviews.

When you fill out the second page on their "Strengths" and "Improvement opportunities," the most important thing you can do is tie your feedback to their earlier performance by paying close attention to what they did this time versus the last time you worked with them. Were they more hypothesis-driven and less generic than last time? Did they brainstorm 7 ideas instead of 1 like they did the last time? Point those contrasts and relative improvements out. Recognize their hard work.

Or did you tell them to be less generic last time but they were still generic this time? In that case, let them know that you've noticed a trend where they are underperforming in this one specific way consistently, and that they can most quickly improve by doubling-down on that area in their solo practice.

Regarding the second goal about making people enjoy working with you, it's important to be mindful of people's egos. We all have egos, so make sure you are encouraging and kind when you deliver feedback. Point out strengths along with improvement opportunities. Though your partner may not request it, if you can provide them with written notes after every session, that may be even more helpful for them.

If you can provide good feedback, you will improve your ability to provide yourself with feedback and your own understanding of the Problem-Solving Process. You'll also do a better job of learning from your partner's strengths. Providing good feedback will likewise increase the probability that people will connect you with their other case practice partners, so assign importance to providing effective feedback.

Section 9-4 Should you get a coach?

I have to share a disclaimer here that I am a case interview coach, so that will bias my perspective on this question. Therefore, I'll share the pros and cons of getting a case interview coach and leave the decision on whether to get one to you.

First, the pros of getting a case interview coach:

- Diagnostic accuracy. Perhaps the most important reason to have a coach is that they can accurately tell you if your performance is above or below the bar.
- Feedback quality. A coach has a depth of experience with providing feedback for improving case interview performance. Their feedback will highlights trends in your performance such as general strengths and weaknesses, and their feedback will be prescriptive, meaning they can tell you specific things you should do to improve.
- Case interview knowledge. A coach has more knowledge of the case interview than your partners. They can share tidbits of information here and there that can prove valuable. If you prepare questions for them, you have a lot to gain in the way of knowledge.
- Accountability. When a coach tells you to work harder, you're more likely to listen than if your friend tells you because you paid a coach a lot of money. If you don't listen to their advice, then you are admitting to yourself that you wasted your money. This accountability factor proves to be valuable for some people who otherwise may procrastinate working on ways to improve their case interview skills.

Now I'll lay out the cons:

- Expensive. Coaching hourly rates can range from $69 to $247. It could give you a huge return-on-investment (ROI), but it also may give you no ROI. You need to manage the risk.
- No guarantee. Not all coaches are effective. When I was going through the interview process, I worked with plenty of coaches who did not help me.

You can mitigate these two cons, however. Regarding coaching being expensive, I'd recommend waiting until a consulting firm invites you to interview. Then try to maximize the probability that you get an offer and therefore a high ROI from your coaching investment by taking a proactive approach to your own preparation. Ask your coach for homework assignments and do that homework beyond what they asked of you. Ask your coach to use the feedback template included in this chapter and understand why they gave you certain ratings. Then take action to improve on their feedback by yourself and make sure that action is sufficient.

Regarding the "no guarantee" con, ask your friends to refer coaches to you they liked. Do your research about certain coaches before you sign up with them, e.g., have they written any blog posts that reveal their approach to feedback, coaching, and the case interview? Are there any reviews written about them on the internet across various coaching websites? If so, see if you can also reach out to the reviewer to ask them questions about that coach's style of coaching.

In your various methods of research, your goal is to see how well the coach scores on the general pros of getting coaching: diagnostic accuracy (do they accurately diagnose whether performance is above the bar?); feedback quality (does their feedback help clients improve?); case interview knowledge (do they have helpful insights about the case interview?); accountability (are they effective at getting their clients to take action that improves their performance?).

Armed with this knowledge, you can decide whether a coach is the right option for you.

Section 9-5 Number of mock case interviews to do per week

I'd recommend that you put yourself through 2 to 5 simulated mock interviews per week as the interviewee. Any less than 2 would be insufficient practice of the rhythm and communication of the case interview, and infrequent feedback for guiding your solo practice. Over 5 would leave you with insufficient time dedicated to solo deliberate practice.

Try to practice regularly with multiple people so you get exposed to different styles of interviewers and different perspectives on your performance. Consider finding 2 to 5 partners who you can practice with once every week.

Jot down a few notes from each mock interview about which areas you need to focus on so you can use those notes to inform your training regimen. For example, did your case practice partner for 2 consecutive interviews tell you that your math seemed to be difficult to follow? Then increase the frequency with which you practice math by yourself.

I know that when I went through the preparation process the first time around, I focused on the number of mock interviews that I should hit, but that was a mistake. The volume of practice does not matter. If you practice more, but you are practicing negative habits, then your practice is hurting you. You need to be deliberate in your practice and mindful of your weaknesses so you can develop an approach to improve them.

If you've followed the advice in this book so far, you'll have developed your case interview skills to the level needed to get an interview offer. But just like an athlete, there's one last component for peak performance, and that is your mindset on game-day. In the next chapter we'll discuss what you can do to be in the right mindset on the day of your interview.

CHAPTER 10

Performance on interview day

"Our mission is to help our clients make distinctive, lasting, and substantial improvements in their performance..."–McKinsey & Company, opening sentence of Mission Statement [8]

Section 10-1 Mindset

I opened the chapter with this cliché mission statement from McKinsey because adopting the client-focused mindset going into my interview was the one critical thing that made all the difference for me between being anxious versus being confident. Before, I had the feelings one would have going into an exam where you're on the spot to arrive at the one right answer, and it's win or lose, all or nothing. That's an attitude that can be nerve-wracking.

What made the difference was when I started pretending that the client in the hypothetical case interview was an actual client who I genuinely wanted to help. I had developed problem-solving skills such as structuring, quantitative analysis, and so on, and I just wanted to bring the best of my abilities to help this client. There was no right or wrong answer, just an application of my skill set to help someone else to the best of my ability.

Ask yourself, are you treating the case interview as an all-or-nothing exam? Or are you treating it as an opportunity to do your best with your developed problem-solving skills to help your client? The former will make you a nervous wreck. The latter will make you enjoy your interview day and perform with confidence.

In addition, take pressure off yourself by remembering that the outcome of your interview day in the broader scheme of your life is most likely going to be immaterial or at most, minor. I know that to be true for the following reasons:

(1) **Repeat application potential**: as I discussed in Section 1-1, I was offered a role at McKinsey a year after they initially turned me down based on my final round interview performance. In addition, at least 20% of my clients are repeat applicants. Consulting firms value repeat applicants.
(2) **Identical potential from other consulting firms**: based on my exit from McKinsey and years since, I've seen many examples of consultants from more prestigious consulting firms reporting to a boss who exited a less prestigious consulting firm; or being beaten out for a role by a competing candidate from a less prestigious consulting firm. It is the quality and kind of experience you gain in consulting that determines the types of roles you exit into rather than the prestige of the consulting firm that you exit from.
(3) **Greater life satisfaction from alternate routes**: from posts in online forums that I had access to while in consulting, I know that a large percentage (if not most) consultants at McKinsey are not happy because of the long hours, travel, and high levels of stress. The same is likely true of other consulting firms. For me personally, I appreciate being able to pursue excellence in my hobbies such as rock climbing (a demanding hobby) that a non-consulting career affords me. If you don't get the opportunity to work at one of these consulting firms, you should view it as a positive for your life satisfaction.

No matter what, the case interview skills you developed through this process will be valuable to you in your strategic decision making. In order to make sure you don't get stressed out about being stressed out, remember that anxiety and stress are actually positive in that they generate adrenaline and energy that we'll discover in Section 10-6 is actually a good thing.

Let's deep-dive into some specific drivers of anxiety on interview day.

Section 10-2 "Stress" interviews

So-called "stress" interviews are those during which the interviewer behaves in a way to make you anxious, such as being confrontational, providing negative feedback, or being difficult in some other way to throw you off. Although some interview preparation sources exaggerate these stories, it does happen regularly that interviewers will be difficult in a way that generates anxiety in candidates.

First, I'll share the things that interviewers do to be difficult. I think of them as falling into one of two categories: non-verbal negative feedback, and verbal negative feedback.

Non-verbal negative feedback

The non-verbal negative feedback is what you will encounter the most frequently. In fact, I'd say that most of my case interview coaching clients will encounter this behavior with one interviewer during every round of interviews. That means that if it is a first-round interview with two interviewers, I'd expect one of the two to display non-verbal negative feedback. If it's a final round interview with four interviewers, I'd still expect one interviewer to display non-verbal negative feedback. You need to prepare mentally for this kind of behavior on every interview day.

This behavior manifests itself in the interviewer being very unenthusiastic about you. They will respond to your answers in a manner that makes you feel as if you aren't being engaging. They will maintain a neutral facial expression throughout the interview. Further, they will behave in a manner to make you feel that you failed the interview during the interview and afterwards.

The way you need to handle these interviewers is to do the challenging task of refraining from making any conclusions about your performance! Ignore the non-verbal negative feedback you are receiving and continue to do your best in the interview and in any subsequent interviews that day. In my experience, that of my coaching clients, and that of friends, candidates will pass the interview even when they felt that one interviewer did not like them, and even if that one interviewer represented half of the people that interviewed them that day! The danger of letting negative feedback get into your head is that it can throw you off your game during that interview and even worse, in subsequent interviews.

Verbal negative feedback

Verbal negative feedback is something that happens more often in McKinsey's interviews than those from other firms in my experience. It will occur during the PEI (personal experience interview). The interviewer will ask for a story that shows a certain soft skill. When the interviewee provides a story in response, the interviewer will respond by saying that they don't think this story is appropriate, and will ask if the interviewee can think of something else.

This kind of request to change the story is negative feedback that can be disorienting for some interviewees. But don't take it too negatively. I know from experience that receiving this kind of feedback happens frequently and rarely ever means that you are not performing well. It only means that the interviewer wants to help you make sure you are providing them with the best story to highlight the particular strength they are trying to learn about.

My advice is to work with the interviewer to find a good story. And as with non-verbal negative feedback, be sure to not draw any conclusions about your performance. Stay focused and stay confident.

Section 10-3 Q&A and small talk etiquette with interviewers

Your asking the interviewer questions and the small talk between the two of you are opportunities where the interviewer is assessing your cultural fit with their firm. They're thinking, "what kinds of things have interested this candidate so far and what are they interested in learning more about?"

My advice here is to think through why you want to go into consulting. What do you want out of your time in consulting? What questions come out of that thought process that you'd want to learn more about that this interviewer may answer for you.

For example, in my case as someone coming from a PhD background, I was curious about how PhD's develop in consulting, what strengths they already bring, and how much their soft skills improve. I would ask this kind of question to a more junior consultant in the first round who either has a PhD themselves or who has worked closely with PhDs in consulting. I think that demonstrated to my interviewers that I would fit in well with the feedback-focused culture at McKinsey and that I would be open to and take feedback seriously in order to develop my soft skills that PhD's don't come in with. Everyone has distinct things they're interested in learning more about, so think through yours. It may interest you to learn about opportunities to do consulting engagements abroad, so ask about that.

I want to emphasize that you want to ask questions appropriate for the audience. I would never ask a partner or senior partner in the final round about what it's like to work with a PhD because at their level, their peers are not freshly minted PhD's. Instead I would ask them about some idea or trend that I find interesting in their industry of expertise. For example, I'd ask a partner who is focused on oil and gas about recent news involving OPEC. (When I interviewed in the Houston office, I suspected that I'd encounter an oil and gas partner, so I had been reading oil and gas news in the preceding days).

Pay close attention to the background of your interviewer from the biographical information you receive prior to your interview and when they introduce themselves to you. Then try to intersect your interests with their experiences. Another one of my interviewers specialized in public sector work. Public sector was something I wanted to get involved with, but it wasn't at the top of my list. I admitted to him I didn't know much about McKinsey's work in the public sector, but that I was interested in learning more if there was anything he could share with me. We ended up having a fascinating discussion about work that McKinsey was doing in Colombia.

Section 10-4 Video and phone interviews

Often consulting firms will require you to pass an initial screening interview through video or phone before they will interview you in person. The two categories of differences you need to account for with these channels are first, technical problems, and second, poor quality communication.

Unlike in the in-person interview, when you are interviewing through video or phone, you become responsible for a certain scope of the logistics: the connection on your side, your equipment, and the venue where you take the call. Make sure you account for at least 10 minutes before the interview to smooth over any technical issues like your phone line or camera not working. If you can test your equipment the day before, that's even better. These precautions will make your interview experience smoother and much less stressful.

Second, when you are using video or phone, the quality of the communication becomes poorer. The audio limitations can create miscommunications between you and the interviewer. And the limited field of view, or absence of video altogether, eliminates the critical visual channel for facilitating your communications.

To manage the audio limitations, make it a point to not hesitate to ask for clarifications and for your interviewer to repeat information. If you miss one phrase that the interviewer shared that has a key piece of

Determine questions to ask your interviewer by intersecting your interests with their background and focus areas

Round of interview	Sample relevant interests to you	Relevant interviewer background and/or current focus areas	Resulting question topics
1st round	• Strengths and weaknesses of your background at the firm (e.g., for undergrads, MBAs, advanced degree holders)	• Usually relatively fresh out of school and working with others who are as well from different educational backgrounds	• "What natural strengths and weaknesses do PhD's bring to consulting?"
	• Working on projects abroad	• May have worked abroad	• "Tell me more about your China work"
	• Skills developed working in consulting	• Early career so will be focused on personal growth	• "What's been the most important skill you've developed in consulting?"
	• Client impact	• Usually striving for client impact	• "Tell me about typical client impact"
Final round	• Recent news in certain industries	• Expert in a specific industry	• "Thoughts on AMC and Universal recent agreement on streaming?"
	• Trends in certain functions	• Expert in a specific function	• "Do you think that healthcare is the slowest industry to adopt Digital?"
	• How the firm leadership thinks about its culture and values	• May be involved in certain committees dictating firm policies	• "What does your role on the partner selection committee entail?"
	• The specific office you're interviewing with	• May be involved as office leader setting office culture	• "What specific initiatives is the Office pursuing independently of the firm?"

ONSIGHT CASE INTERVIEW COACHING

Onsightcasecoaching.com
manu@onsightcasecoaching.com

Figure 10-1 Guide for deciding on what questions you should ask your interviewers.

information, it will hamper your ability to drive insights. If you think you missed a phrase, ask the interviewer to repeat it.

To manage the limited video field of view during a video interview, make it a point to lift your notes to show them to the interviewer in the camera whenever you present to them your structures or your math tables. If the resolution of the video is not sufficient for your interviewer to make out your notes, they may ask you to not bother showing them your notes, in which case, follow the advice I'll share for phone interviews.

In the absence of video altogether—in phone interviews or video interviews with limited resolution—make it a point to use clear language to describe what is on your notes. For example, you can say, "On my notes here, I have 2 rows, one for before we invest in the new technology, and one for after we invest in the new technology. I will add rows for each step of the calculation now. My first row is the variable cost...". Another example would be, "I am now moving to the 2nd bucket of my structure on my page, which is Costs. Under costs, I have 3 sub-buckets...". This way your interviewer will visualize the structure and be able to follow your logic with clarity.

Section 10-5 First-round versus final-round interview days

Once you pass your first round, you'll find yourself thinking about whether to do anything differently to prepare for the next round of interviews. The reason that consulting firms have multiple rounds of interviews is to manage the cost of their recruiting process by having a screening round conducted by more junior consultants to reduce the volume of candidates that the firm partners have to spend their time interviewing. Otherwise, the consulting firm intends to apply the same criteria and frameworks to testing candidates throughout their process. They are still intending to test for the same problem-solving skills and soft skills.

That means that your final round does not differ from the first round, except that your interviewers are more senior and that the decisions made on your candidacy at that point are irreversible (meaning that a "pass" in the final round results in the firm committing to you whereas that is not the case in the first round). The implications of the second point on irreversibility means that the bar or the standard applied to measure your performance in the final round will be higher because the firm has to commit to you at that point. First round interviewers, when they pass a candidate, are passing the buck to the partners and the office who conduct the final round interview on that candidate so they will subconsciously let things slide a little more. Recognizing the greater importance of the final round, consulting firms require a greater number of interviews in the final round than the first round.

What does this mean for you and how should you prepare differently in between rounds?

1. Since you know that you need to get even better, I recommend that you get in touch with your first-round interviewers to ask their feedback and advice for how you can improve based on their impressions of you.
2. Brace yourself for more of the "stress" interviews described in Section 10-2. They are even more likely to occur with more senior interviewers.
3. Prepare to ask different kinds of questions of these more senior interviewers, such as about their industries or their roles on internal committees leading their firm. You can get their biographies from your recruiter earlier than you could for the first round. Also listen to them introduce themselves for indications of client-focus and internal firm-building committee work.
4. Mentally and physically prepare for a longer day of interviews, which we turn to now.

Section 10-6 Marathon interview days

Many consulting firms will have around 4 hours of consecutive interviews for the final round. In the past I've been concerned about whether I could maintain my energy level to have peak performance on all 4 interviews.

Preparation for the final round involves 4 key differences from the first round

	1st round interviews	Final round interviews	How to prepare
1 Higher bar	Reversible decision: by passing you, the firm is not making any irreversible commitments to you	Irreversible decision: because a pass in this case involves a significant commitment, interviews subconsciously set a higher bar for your performance	Request feedback from your 1st round interviews and focus on improving in those areas while maintaining your existing strengths
2 Stress interviews	Junior interviews: it's easier to form a natural rapport with a more junior interviewer because they were more recently in your shoes.	Senior interviewers: because they are farther removed from being in your shoes, more senior interviewers are more likely to display detached body language.	Mentally prepare yourself to overlook signs of negative feedback such as uninterested body language and putting you on the spot to answer questions w/o time to think.
3 Rapport through Q&A	Generalists: more junior interviewers are unlikely to have specialized in an area in consulting.	Specialists: more senior interviewers are more likely to have an industry/function or internal firm-building activity they're passionate about.	In the first round, ask more general questions about the interviewer's experience. In the final round, get the interviewer to talk about their specialized passion in consulting.
4 Long interview days	2 hours: first rounds are shorter because of their non-committal nature.	3-4 hours: due to the irreversibility of the decision, final rounds tend to be longer assessments.	Mentally and physically prepare for the longer day. Have some snacks ready to go for breaks in between interviews.

Figure 10-2 Differences between the first and final round of case interviews.

There are two things in my experience that will carry you through: adrenaline and nourishment.

I've been through these kinds of 4+ hour interview days multiple times. The day of my final round with McKinsey that ended successfully, I did not sleep much the night before. Adrenaline and excitement about the opportunity at hand made the lack of sleep a non-issue. So my first piece of advice for you about approaching marathon interview days is not worry about them because the adrenaline and preparation you've already done will carry you through.

Even with adrenaline, nourishment is important for 4 consecutive hours of interviews. Besides having a substantial breakfast, you might pack a protein bar in your bag that you can take a bite of in between interviews during your bathroom breaks. If coffee does not make you too anxious, consider sipping on it during your interviews. All consulting offices will have a kitchen with a coffee machine that you can ask your interviewer or the recruiter to help you find and learn how to use.

Epilogue

"For the past 33 years, I have looked in the mirror every morning and asked myself: 'If today were the last day of my life, would I want to do what I am about to do today?' And whenever the answer has been 'No' for too many days in a row, I know I need to change something."–Steve Jobs commencement address at Stanford University, June 12, 2005 [31]

I'd seen Steve Jobs's commencement address at Stanford University on YouTube countless times, but it wasn't until after I applied the 7-Step Problem-Solving Process in my case interview preparation that I began to practice his example of looking myself in the mirror every morning and asking if I'd still do what I were about to do that day if I knew that it would be the last of my life. This practice is in effect Step 3 or the "Prioritize Issues" step of the Problem-Solving Process.

But you can only prioritize issues once you lay out your goals for your life (Step 1: "Define Problem") and lay out a plan for achieving your goals (Step 2: "Structure Problem"). For example, if after reflection you've decided that spending time with your family and exercising are among the most important goals in your life, then why isn't that on your agenda for today? Why haven't you prioritized it? Becoming a disciplined problem-solver means focusing on the right things.

Being an effective problem-solver also means working with other people to look at all sides of an issue—whether that be your spouse, a collaborator, or a colleague—to find synergistic solutions. One of my favorite examples of this is a story about Steve Jobs that comes from former Walt Disney CEO Bob Iger [32]. In 2005, when Disney Animation was coming off a decade of losses totaling $400M from producing mediocre films, Iger had the idea that the only way to turn Disney around was to acquire Pixar, which Steve Jobs led. Given Jobs's reputation for exceptional self-confidence, no one on the Disney board--including Iger himself—thought Pixar would agree to being acquired.

To Iger's surprise, when he brought up the possibility over the phone, Jobs welcomed a further discussion. Here I include a few excerpts from Iger that reveal what happened next:

> *A couple of weeks after that call in my driveway, he (Steve Jobs) and I met in Apple's boardroom in Cupertino, California. Steve said he loved whiteboard exercises, where an entire vision—all the thoughts and designs and calculations—could be drawn out. He stood with marker in hand and scrawled PROS on one side and CONS on the other. "You start," he said. "Got any pros?" Two hours later, the pros were meager, and the cons were abundant, even if a few of them, in my estimation, were quite petty. "A few solid pros are more powerful than dozens of cons," Steve said. "So what should we do next?" Another lesson: Steve was great at weighing all sides of an issue.*

Media coverage has caricatured Jobs to seem like an opinionated know-it-all. In this story, we see however that he was capable of inclusive problem-solving. In this example, he led Iger through the structured brainstorming exercise that I laid out in Section 4-3.

Disney went on to acquire Pixar in 2006. After the acquisition, Disney successfully preserved the creative culture at Pixar, as Pixar continued producing hit films such as *Inside Out*, *Up*, and *Brave* following the Disney acquisition. The two companies also generated revenue synergies by incorporating the characters, intellectual property, and branding from those successful Pixar films into Disney's theme parks, resorts, and merchandise businesses. If you purchased $100 of Disney stock on January 1st, 2005 (well before the Pixar acquisition) and held it until January 1st,

2014, the value of your holding would have grown to $5,973. Compare that to if you invested the $100 in the S&P500 index, in which case your holding would have only grown to $1,575 over the same period.

I want to remind you that you are developing a skill set that will have a positive impact on the people touched by the organizations that you will become involved with. As an example, the last story I want to share with you is how the application of a rigorous problem-solving approach in a time of international discord prevented what most people alive at the time expected would inevitably lead to World War III.

The Cuban Missile Crisis in October 1962—during the Cold War—was set off when the Soviet Union secretly placed ballistic missiles in Cuba, a position from which they could attack much of the United States. The military leaders in the United States pressured President John Kennedy—because of the shift in strategic balance that the missiles positioned in Cuba created and the risk of nuclear attack that it posed—to launch air attacks and an invasion to destroy the missiles. Congressional leaders piled on pressure on Kennedy to invade Cuba.

Kennedy had learned from his earlier mistake in supporting the Bay of Pigs invasion to not blindly trust the recommendations of military experts. Therefore, he decided that since he did not have the same subject matter expertise as the military experts, that he would have to use a rigorous problem-solving approach along with a committee of advisors. Quoting from Robert Dallek's *An Unfinished Life* [33], we know that Kennedy used the "Define Problem" step to focus his committee:

> *The first order of business was not to assign blame for the Soviet-American confrontation but to find some way to eliminate the missiles and avert a nuclear war.*

We learn that Kennedy structured the problem to have four potential options that each needed to be further investigated:

> *For the moment, Kennedy was not thinking about any political or diplomatic solution; his focus was on military options and how to*

mute the crisis until they had some clear idea of what to do. He saw four possible military actions: an air strike against the missile installations; a more general air attack against a wide array of targets; a blockade; and an invasion.

We know that by Day 3 of the crisis after a series of meetings with various leaders and advisors, that Kennedy along with his brother Bobby were going along with an iterative problem-solving approach, as they had revised their upfront structure for next steps to include 5 options:

At midnight, after three long meetings, Bobby summarized five options that advisers were putting before the president.

President Kennedy continued to use a hypothesis-driven approach by having a "preference" while pursuing next steps to gather data to test that preference before taking action:

Kennedy had not ruled out military action, but his remarks at the meetings on October 18 revealed a preference for a blockade and negotiations. He wanted to know (i.e., he wanted data to test his hypothesis)...

He had leaders present more information on the various sides of the options as well:

Advocates of an air strike and a blockade formed themselves into committees to develop their respective arguments.

Kennedy and his advisors arrived at the plan to pursue a combination of a blockade of Cuba and diplomacy with the Soviet Union. The US implemented the blockade on October 22nd and the Soviet Union capitulated to removing the missiles from Cuba on October 28th. The significance of the event is best captured by Dallek:

> *Forty years after the crisis, historians almost uniformly agree that this was the most dangerous moment in the forty-five-year Cold War. Kennedy's restraint in resisting a military solution that would almost certainly have triggered a nuclear exchange makes him a model of wise statesmanship in a dire situation. One only need compare his performance with that of Europe's heads of government before World War I—a disaster that cost millions of lives and wasted unprecedented sums of wealth.*

Like questions of war and peace, you will face many strategic decisions in your life and work. When you approach them, I hope you do so with disciplined thought and clarity.

Bibliography

[1]	K. Bryant, "The Lakers retire Kobe Bryant's No. 8 and No. 24 | Ceremony & Speeches | NBA on ESPN," ESPN, 18 December 2017. [Online]. Available: https://www.youtube.com/watch?v=t2ONe8N6x0Q. [Accessed 14 April 2020].
[2]	W. S. Jr and E. B. White, The Elements of Style, New York: Macmillan, 1959.
[3]	B. G. Malkiel and C. D. Ellis, The Elements of Investing, Hoboken, New Jersey: John Wiley & Sons, 2010.
[4]	J. F. Kennedy, "COMMENCEMENT ADDRESS AT AMERICAN UNIVERSITY, WASHINGTON, D.C., JUNE 10, 1963," 10 June 1963. [Online]. Available: https://www.jfklibrary.org/archives/other-resources/john-f-kennedy-speeches/american-university-19630610. [Accessed 5 April 2020].
[5]	McKinsey & Company, "How to master the seven-step problem-solving process," 19 September 2019. [Online]. Available: https://www.mckinsey.com/business-functions/strategy-and-corporate-finance/our-insights/how-to-master-the-seven-step-problem-solving-process. [Accessed March 2020].
[6]	R. M. Charles Conn, Bulletproof Problem Solving: The One Skill That Changes Everything, 1, Ed., Wiley, 2019.
[7]	J. Hubbard, "Jordan on Jordan: MJ REFLECTS ON THE CHALLENGES AHEAD," HOOP MAGAZINE, April 1997. [Online]. Available: http://archive.nba.com/jordan/hoop_mjonmj.html. [Accessed 5 April 2020].
[8]	McKinsey & Company, "Our mission and values," [Online]. Available: https://www.mckinsey.com/about-us/overview/our-mission-and-values. [Accessed 5 April 2020].

[9]	McKinsey & Company, "Electro-Light Practice Case," [Online]. Available: https://www.mckinsey.com/careers/interviewing/electrolight. [Accessed 27 March 2020].
[10]	McKinsey & Company, "GlobaPharm Practice Case," [Online]. Available: https://www.mckinsey.com/careers/interviewing/globapharm. [Accessed 27 March 2020].
[11]	MIT Sloan Management Consulting Club, "2015-2016 Recruiting Case book," [Online]. Available: https://www.scribd.com/document/435795464/MIT515828010-pdf. [Accessed 2 April 2020].
[12]	University of Texas McCombs School of Business, "Town Mayor Case," [Online]. Available: https://kupdf.net/download/2015-16-student-casebook-pdf_58dc7d98dc0d60bf34897102_pdf. [Accessed 2 April 2020].
[13]	Duke The Fuqua School of Business, "The Duke MBA Consulting Club Casebook 2016-2017," [Online]. Available: https://careerinconsulting.com/wp-content/uploads/2019/12/11.-Fuqua-Case-book-2017.pdf. [Accessed 2 April 2020].
[14]	G. Beahm, I, Steve: Steve Jobs In His Own Words, Agate Publishing, 2011.
[15]	Wikipedia, "Amazon HQ2," [Online]. Available: https://en.wikipedia.org/wiki/Amazon_HQ2. [Accessed 24 April 2020].
[16]	Boston Consulting Group, "What Is the Growth Share Matrix?," [Online]. Available: https://www.bcg.com/about/our-history/growth-share-matrix.aspx. [Accessed 24 April 2020].
[17]	G. E. P. Box, "Science and Statistics," *Journal of the American Statistical Association,* vol. 71, no. 356, pp. 791-799, 1976.
[18]	Ross School of Business Consulting Club, "Casebook 2008 - Ross Consulting Club," [Online]. Available: https://wenku.baidu.com/view/1d44af5d53d380eb6294dd88d0d233d4b14e3f2f.html?re=view. [Accessed 2 April 2020].
[19]	Yale Graduate Student Consulting Club, "Case Book 2013," September 2013. [Online]. Available: https://pdfslide.net/documents/yale-casebook-2013-full-6.html. [Accessed 2 April 2020].

[20]	Kellogg Consulting Club, "Case Book and Interview Guide | 2012 edition," 2012. [Online]. Available: https://www.caseinterview.com/wp-content/uploads/2019/08/Kellogg-2012.pdf. [Accessed 2 April 2020].
[21]	Investopedia, "Rule of 72 Definition," 6 March 2020. [Online]. Available: https://www.investopedia.com/terms/r/ruleof72.asp. [Accessed 25 April 2020].
[22]	W. Bogdanich and M. Forsythe, "How We've Reported on the Secrets and Power of McKinsey & Company," *The New York Times,* 19 February 2019.
[23]	J. Collins, Good to Great: Why Some Companies Make the Leap...And Others Don't, William Collins, 2001.
[24]	Wall Street Oasis, "Make Your Case: Master Consulting Case Interviewers," 2014. [Online]. Available: https://www.coursehero.com/file/p4g7hhsg/Push-the-candidate-to-be-creative-and-think-of-five-different-property-uses/. [Accessed 6 April 2020].
[25]	SpeakingSherpa, "How to Tell a Business Story Using the McKinsey Situation-Complication-Resolution (SCR) Framework," 18 November 2017. [Online]. Available: https://speakingsherpa.com/how-to-tell-a-business-story-using-the-mckinsey-situation-complication-resolution-scr-framework/. [Accessed 5 April 2020].
[26]	J. Eig, Ali: A Life, Houghton Mifflin Harcourt, 2017.
[27]	C-SPAN, "Secretary of State Nominee Announcement," 21 December 2012. [Online]. Available: https://www.c-span.org/video/?310073-1/secretary-state-nominee-announcement. [Accessed 9 April 2020].
[28]	Duke APD Consulting Club, "Duke APD Consulting Club homepage," [Online]. Available: https://sites.duke.edu/dukeapdconsulting/. [Accessed 9 April 2020].
[29]	McKinsey & Company, "Insight 2020," [Online]. Available: https://www.mckinsey.com/careers/students/insight/overview. [Accessed 9 April 2020].

[30]	Boston Consulting Group, "Bridge to BCG Consulting Workshop," [Online]. Available: https://www.bcg.com/en-us/careers/students/adc-bridge-to-bcg.aspx. [Accessed 9 April 2020].
[31]	S. Jobs, "Steve Jobs' 2005 Stanford Commencement Address," Stanford University, 12 June 2005. [Online]. Available: https://www.youtube.com/watch?v=UF8uR6Z6KLc. [Accessed 15 April 2020].
[32]	R. Iger, The Ride of a Lifetime: Lessons Learned from 15 Years as CEO of the Walt Disney Company, Random House, 2019.
[33]	R. Dallek, An Unfinished Life: John F. Kennedy 1917-1963, Little, Brown and Company, 2003.

Glossary

7-Step Problem-Solving Process (or the Problem-Solving Process): the set of steps articulated by McKinsey for guiding how its consultants approach client engagements. The 7 steps are laid out in Figure 2-1.

B2B: business-to-business, where the client company's customers are organizations rather than people.

B2C: business-to-consumer, where the client company's customers are end-consumers or individual people as opposed to organizations.

Brainstorming: a skill or question in the case interview that tests the candidate's creativity. Involves asking the candidate to suggest creative potential solutions to a question. Solutions need not be accurate or tested but only serve as potential ideas for further discussion. Along with Exhibit Interpretation, makes up the Conceptual Problem-Solving skill.

Case: the overall hypothetical scenario that is the topic of the case interview.

Case interview: interview focused on exploring how the candidate approaches solving an open-ended problem, a hypothetical problem usually in a business-setting for a client.

Clarifying questions: the phase of the case interview following the interviewer's reading of the case background. The interviewer will give the Interviewee an opportunity during this stage to ask questions to better understand the context. This phase precedes the interviewee's opportunity to develop an upfront structure.

Exhibit interpretation: a skill or question in the case interview that tests the candidate's ability to use data to further the thinking about the case, such as by making insightful observations, proposing hypotheses, proposing next steps, or reaching conclusions or recommendations. Along with Brainstorming, makes up the Conceptual Problem-Solving skill.

Final recommendation: a skill or question in the case interview at the end of the interview where the interviewer will ask for a brief synthesis or summary that you would give the CEO or another leader at the client.

Generic framework: a framework that is intended to be broadly applicable to a category of client scenarios and that therefore should be memorized and applied as needed.

Hypothesis-driven: laying out several hypotheses as the rationale when laying out structures, plans, or questions.

Interviewee-led: case interview format where the interviewer opens with a general problem context and then expects the interviewee to take the lead. Interviewer will answer questions that the interviewee asks but expects the interviewee to determine the next stages of conversation.

Interviewer-led: case interview format where the interviewer guides the interviewee through a series of questions and waits for a response for each before moving on to the next question. Some consulting firms such as McKinsey employ this format instead of the interviewee-led format.

M&A: mergers and acquisitions, which is a functional category of consulting engagement dealing with scenarios that involve one company acquiring another, or two companies executing a merger after the acquisition.

MECE: Mutually Exclusive and Collectively Exhaustive, which is a preferred feature for structures. A structure that is MECE does not contain overlapping buckets (i.e., categories) and its buckets encompass all plausible solutions.

Onsight Case System®: the 3-pillar approach to preparing for the case interview that forms the foundation of this book, i.e., problem-solving, habits of communication, and training. I lay out the Onsight Case System® in Figure 1-1.

Quantitative questions: a skill or question in the case interview that tests the candidate's ability to structure an approach to build a financial model, obtain and apply data, and conduct computation.

Slide: a visual aid in the form of a graphic. In the case interview, your notes are slides. Consultants' principal products are slides, so assign high importance to slide-making in the case interview.

Structure: a disaggregation (comprising 5 or fewer items) approach that you or your team will use for organizing subsequent analysis. Items of disaggregation can be in the form of categorical or chronological phases of analysis.

Thought leader: the person who moves the thinking of the team forward to achieve more. This forward movement can take place through being hypothesis-driven, laying out plans, or anticipating issues that need to be thought through.

Upfront structure: structure for the overall case that you provide at the beginning after asking clarifying questions.

VOM: acronym for clarifying questions–value chain, objective, money.

Index

N

O

P

Q

Made in the USA
Middletown, DE
08 May 2021